# THE
# IMAM
## AND THE
# ATHEIST

# THE
# IMAM
## AND THE
# ATHEIST

## MOHAMED
## A. AZEEZ

CLARITAS
BOOKS

1 2 3 4 5 6 7 8 9 10

CLARITAS BOOKS

Bernard Street, Swansea, United Kingdom
Milpitas, California, United States

**CLARITAS**
BOOKS

First Published in August 2023

Typeset in Minion Pro 14/11

The Imam and The Atheist
By Mohamed A. Azeez

Series Editor: Sharif H. Banna

A CIP catalogue record for this book is available from the British Library

ISBN: 978-1-80011-003-8

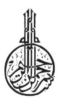

IMAM MOHAMED A. AZEEZ is the Co-Founder and Senior Imam of the Tarbiya Institute in California. He has a multi-disciplinary background in Medicine, Social Sciences and Islamic Theology. With a demonstrated history working with religious institutions, he excels in nonprofit organizational management, fundraising, recruitment, event planning and coaching - with a special focus on youth work. Imam Azeez is trained in both the religious and secular sciences, being a physician and a social scientist by education, and a religious scholar and an Imam by traditional training. With 15 years of experience, Imam Azeez is an eloquent orator who seamlessly blends modern approaches with traditional authenticity. He focuses on propounding a philosophically sound Islamic ethos whereby modern challenges are addressed through an authentic Islamic lens. His alma maters inlcude Ohio State University and the University of Chicago. Imam Azeez resides in Northern California with his family.

# Contents

# Prologue

"Please help me save my son!" are the words that haunted me for months. They poured out of a mother's mouth like lava during a counselling meeting. Her son was not lost to drugs or gangs but rather, to the atheist club at his college. Her son, as the mother described, was religious, talented, insightful, and loving. But in her words, "he was lost to the wolves". I can't remember how many young people have lost their faith in our community over the last five years. Neither can I remember how many sleepless nights I've had over it. As someone who has had his share of faith struggles growing up, I can relate to the experience of a young person who has lost his faith. But as a religious leader, and a parent, I live in daily horror for fear of losing another young person, or one of my own, to the abysmal trap of atheism. After all, who wants to lose a child to the proverbial wolf?

This fear propelled me on a journey that I have been treading for years: to study the literature of atheism, and to formulate strong arguments to help my children cope and resist. I say my children because that is the sole reason that compelled me to embark upon this path. Most of our conversations at the dinner table would have less to do with how things went at school, or what transpired at karate practice. Rather, Descartes, Hume and Kant were habitual dinner guests. We probably spoke more about Aristotle, Aquinas and Ghazali, than we spoke about Trump, Sisi, or the Coronavirus. An Imam is expected to spend most of his time teaching his kids religious piety, instilling in their hearts the importance of prayer, or getting them to memorise their Quran. But piety is moot when the mind is restless. Helping my kids sail their intellectual boats to the shores of safety took priority over pretending that the ocean is stormless. And as we engaged together, our bonds grew stronger. The walks we took, the discussions we had, and the book readings we covered, in the end, seeing my kids' faith in God growing, and noticing how their minds are gradually shielded from unmitigated atheistic discourse, made the journey absolutely worthwhile. It seemed that the wolves lost one round at least.

But it was this sequence of events that inspired this book project.

As the intensity of community feedback about atheism grew, and as the number of young people that lost their faith skyrocketed, it became clear to me that something needs to be done. The conventional methods of youth work - bringing teenagers to a regular meeting or putting them in a weekly *halaqa* - seemed not only insufficient but rather harmful, as they ignore open wounds and make false assumptions about where people's hearts are. It became painfully apparent to me that a fresh and perhaps unusual approach was necessary. The Imam who's busy all day putting out fires and managing disputes, needs to actually achieve the arduous task of setting time aside to develop a well-thought-out solution to help young Muslims muscle their way through the stampede of atheism. What an uphill battle! But then I realised something. The lengthy conversations I had with my children, the back and forth, the arguments and their rebuttals, the moments of parental triumph and sheer defeat, all contributed to the creation of long dialogues that usually ended with preserving the idea of God. If only I could recapture those dialogues and put them on paper! And then it dawned on me. Instead of engaging in workshops, seminars, events, speeches, and other activities that give Imams what they lust for the most - preaching - perhaps time is needed to be carved out of the daily grind to actually write. Write? Initially, it was a horrifying prospect. But when I realised that the material was already there, the undertaking became a lot less frightening.

And so the project began. Inking down conversation after conversation, with their emotions, sentiments, back and forth, arguments and counter-arguments, for the purpose of bringing to light that the human mind can, on its own, affirm the existence of the Creator. A dialogue format was an exhilarating idea because it enabled me to include possible responses to my arguments and how to refute them and to breathe some life into what could otherwise be a tedious discourse.

In classical times, Plato captured his teacher Socrates' ideas in his timeless work, The Republic, where a fictitious conversation between Socrates and a curious man took the reader through an incredible journey about justice and what an ideal society should look like. This book project will be modelled after this design. A conversation starts between an Imam (not me in particular) and a community member who has supposedly lost his nephew to atheism. Through the dialogue, the Imam weaves his arguments to help the man cope, but concurrently finds creative ways to help the nephew return to the fold. In this dialogue, the Imam not only covers arguments for God made by philosophers throughout the ages but also takes shots at atheistic arguments, using logic and science.

But is this even a possible task? To use philosophical enquiry and scientific perspectives to prove the unproven? Perhaps I need to expound on this a bit further.

It is often suggested that once one applies the rigorous methods of science or the logical means of reason, that God will shatter on the rocks of reality. This doesn't explain, however, why most philosophers and scientists, at least until the last century, were believers. From Socrates, Plato and Aristotle, through Spinoza, Locke and Kant, on to Pierce, Putnam and Gardner. Even great scientists, such as Newton, Einstein, Heisenberg, Harvey, and yes, Darwin, were believers. Where did we derive the assumption that science/philosophy on the one hand and religion, on the other hand, were antithetical? How did we come to the conclusion that scientific methods and reason are objective while religious beliefs are subjective and unverifiable? This is an underlying theme that will repeatedly be addressed in this project. Philosophical naturalists, who believe that everything in the universe, including biological life, conscience, morality and feelings are made of material things, would have us accept this paradigm as self-evident.

Yet, it's not subjective to observe that the vast majority of human beings accept a higher power beyond the universe, one way or the other. This conclusion is based on an individual's first-hand experience with what feels real to him/her in every possible way. If this feeling is subjective, then how is it different from philosophical naturalists who believe that there are multiple universes without any verifiable evidence to support their claims? Moreover, believing in a higher power, it is claimed by naturalists, was concocted by the human mind to deal with feelings of loneliness, loss, and purposelessness of the early man. It is a coping mechanism per se, engendered in the human cultural experience to make life more palatable. Believing in God, albeit unfounded, brings serious relief, solace, and comfort to the human experience in a very real sense, even if it stems from fiction rather than reality.

This contention may hold water until one realises that believing in God doesn't always bring comfort and relief. In fact, religious obligations can be cumbersome and tedious, and bring with them a host of dos and don'ts, limitations, and requirements that often make religious people struggle in discomfort. Religiously observant folk often view those who indulge in vices with a modicum of jealousy. Believing in God may come with some short-term gratification, but it also comes with more-than-occasional guilt and remorse when one engages in sinful behaviour. Religious belief by design defers judgement, reward, and punishment to the afterlife. To argue that believers have faith in God because it brings them immediate benefit in the life of this world may seem inapplicable to the majority of believers. Faith compels people to make sacrifices, live with altruism, put others before themselves, focus on the greater good, deny oneself comforts, avoid unbecoming behaviour, and refrain from seeking economic gain and financial success through sinful means. Overall, while believing in a higher power may bring great comfort to believers, the great discipline that it demands makes it certainly more burdensome than not believing. In other words, faith puts believers in a relatively weaker position -materially- vis-a-vis non-believers.

This understanding may slice through the naturalist argument about how men of faith made up religion to bring themselves much-needed comfort. But looking at faith through this lens does a lot more than just that. If one were to take natural selection without a grain of salt, it would have been safe to conclude that time should have weeded out people of faith, since they are weaker and therefore would be eliminated from the genetic pool to the advantage of non-believers who are more likely to take what they can and give nothing in return. The logic of natural selection would suggest that only non-believers would have survived over time. This is clearly not the case. Faith in the world is alive and well, and while the camp of believers may have sustained bruises in recent battles against atheism, the vast majority of humanity remains connected to a higher power. If the naturalist argument, that religion was necessary in ancient times to bring comfort to the first man against feelings of loneliness, insecurity and helplessness is valid, then religion should have faded completely in the age of postmodern success, stability, and security. This is obviously not the case.

We live in a world in which believers cannot afford to lose themselves to the platitudes of the religious dialectic and stand on defensive lines all the time acting like punching bags, taking blows from atheists. On the other hand, philosophic naturalists cannot afford to be dismissive of realities beyond empirical realms either. The truth is simply too precious to be swept under the rug. And this is where I feel that this book project can make a contribution, by welding this chasm between those who blindly believe and those who stubbornly reject.

This project is primarily meant to be a simple utility in the hands of educators, mentors, and parents who might find themselves in a position to respond to questions about faith raised by those under their care or tutelage. It must be read multiple times so the ideas in the book are infused with one's own, and flow naturally to address contentions raised by young people of faith. While the book is obviously written with Muslim perspectives taken for granted, it's suitable for most people of faith, and the arguments, for the most part, can still be useful. In this age, as men and women of faith combat the new atheistic reality, it's our highest priority to first affirm the concept of God.

On the other hand, it's important to note that this book is not thorough enough to directly debate atheists. More conceptual effort, meticulous investigation, and painstaking citations would be required in order to make this project a utility in the hands of those who engage atheism directly. As will become quickly apparent in the course of the book, the dialogue format, while effective in bringing to life complex notions through a dramatic conversation between two men, is not sufficient to build an airtight case against atheism. In a dialogue, it's tedious to provide citations and references. As clarified earlier, the main purpose of this book is to provide shield and ammunition to educators, mentors, and parents of young people who have questions about God.

This book project will consist of 11 chapters. In the first chapter, introductory notions, ideas, and thought processes about the existence of God will be provided, as well as setting the stage for the dialogue between the Imam and the uncle. The second chapter will cover the Teleological Argument for God, in which both design and order will be discussed, suggesting that a universe that is meticulously designed with a pervasive sense of order is not likely to have just built itself. The third chapter will address the Cosmological Argument for God. If the universe is contingent, what caused it to exist? This chapter will also include the famed Ghazali Kalam Cosmological argument. Chapter four will address the Ontological perspective, covering the Ontological Argument of St. Anselm. Chapter five will establish the existence of God through the moral arguments of Kant and other philosophers. Chapter six will address the arguments against God from Darwinism and will provide an alternative perspective on the origin of man to establish the existence of a Maker, while remaining in fidelity to evolution and scientific progress. Chapter seven will use the existence of human reason, in a way that presupposes experiential knowledge as grounds for believing in God. Chapter eight responds to arguments against creation from the stereotypes of predestination, fatalism, and God's will versus. man's free will, the problem of evil etc. Chapter nine covers the LGBTQA+ ethos and how it affects faith. Chapter 10 focuses on the idea of salvation and how it's obtained considering the diversity of religious paths. Chapter 11 offers a conclusion to the dialogue and addresses minor remaining points about God.

I'm indebted to a great many people who helped me develop, propound, write and edit the ideas of this book. My utmost gratitude goes to the Tarbiya Institute, its staff, board members, and brilliant community. Without them, the space needed for this type of creative work to be debated would have been impossible to achieve. I'm also grateful for the amazing students who attended my God and Philosophy class in Roseville, California for their brilliant questions and indispensable feedback. I'm also filled with gratitude to my family, and particularly my three kids, who managed to somehow put up with dad's esoteric interests and cope with his lengthy, tedious conversations. And above all, I'm grateful to All-Mighty God, who enabled me to offer a small utility to help people find Him and feel His presence. Martin Luther King, Jr. said: "Without God, all of our efforts turn to ashes and our sunrise into the darkest of nights".

*Chapter 1*

# Foundations

It has been at least a week since I heard from him last. He's usually keeping me on edge with his incessant questions and poignant enquiries. But one week of silence was alarming. This time, it was me that had to reach out. So I picked up the phone and called him.

"Assalamu alaykum! How have you been?" I asked with excitement.

"Wa alaykum assalam…Alhamdulillah. How are you?" he said woefully.

"I'm doing well. What's with you? I haven't heard from you in a while, and here you are sulking like you just got laid off!" I said jokingly, trying to lighten his mood.

"I know. I haven't been able to do anything lately."

"And why is that?"

"I don't know if I'm ready to talk about it."

"Of course you are. Come on. Share with me what's going on."

"On the phone? Should we meet instead?"

"Just give me the highlights. We can always follow up later."

"Well…it's tough to explain."

"Just start with where it hurts the most."

"Well, there's no way to put this in mild terms, so I'm just going to say it as it is."

"What?" I asked impatiently.

"My nephew, who was like a son to me and I technically raised him…"

"Oh my God, what happened to him?"

"He renounced Islam."

It took me a few seconds to even respond, and then I mumbled: "Oh God…I'm very sorry to hear this".

"Me too…We were very close. I feel responsible. At the same time, I'm very angry."

"Why are you angry?"

"How could he do this to his family and the people that loved him?" he answered wrathfully.

"Do what?" I asked.

"Lose his faith!"

"But you said it yourself: he lost his faith. No one intentionally loses anything. No one deliberately abandons ideals, values, and beliefs that he or she grew up with unless something compelling drove them to."

"Are you saying that he has an excuse?" he asked with muffled anger.

"I'm saying let's be less angry and more compassionate. Let's put our heads together to understand what happened, how it can be corrected, and how to prevent it from happening to his siblings, and other young people if we can help it," I answered.

"I guess I'm still in the anger phase of my grief…"

"We need to snap you out of this."

"How?"

"Well, listen. Instead of beating yourself up about it, you need to realise that losing faith has become one of the most pervasive phenomena of our time. Most people have been rendered disenchanted. The tidal wave is too high. It's like a tsunami, and to be completely honest, we were not prepared for it at all."

"Who's we?" he asked with frustration.

"People of faith, I mean. We were consumed with our internal disagreements and theological debates, revelling in the abstractness of our doctrines, unbeknownst to us that atheism is organising itself as a new false religion that is snatching our kids right and left before our very eyes."

I could imagine him nodding his head in silent agreement, so I continued.

"The reality is that this is bigger than you and I, and all of our institutions combined. Blaming ourselves for failing to anticipate the growing out of control of atheism, is like blaming Blackberry for failing to see that the consumer was going to trade their security for the allure of touchscreens and to voluntarily sign their slavery ownership deeds to Apple and Samsung. Just like the touchscreen phone, atheism as both a manifestation and a shaper of modern popular culture had an addictive seduction that many of us were defenseless against," I said.

"I guess my question is what can I do to bring my nephew back, and what can we do to protect our community from the threat of losing faith?"

"More important than these questions is why people lose their faith in the first place."

"Why is this more important?"

"Because once we know the agent that causes the disease, we can configure the treatment."

"So what causes people to lose their faith?" He asked impatiently.

"What caused your nephew to lose his faith?"

"Well, he says that it's been brewing in his head for a while, but what really triggered him was his inability to reconcile evolution with creation."

"You mean Darwinism with creation," I abruptly responded.

"Is there a difference?" he asked.

"A huge one, but we can talk about that later. You need to know though, that Darwinism is one of the most common causes of people losing their faith. It has been for the last hundred years."

"But I too studied it in high school and just logged it away and never allowed it to affect my faith!"

"Are you able today to resolve the mutually exclusive premises of creationism and Darwinism?"

"Not necessarily."

"Well, that's the thing. Not everyone is capable of just tuning it out!"

"I guess not."

"I told you we are not equipped."

"No kidding…What else drives people to atheism?" he asked inquisitively.

"The intellectual ethos in which Darwinism thrives."

"What is that?"

"Philosophic naturalism, which is the assumption that the universe is just material. Nothing exists out there, so the argument goes, that cannot be processed and explained through the senses, or verified empirically. If a claim cannot be falsified through the empirical method, it's invalid. The metaphysical doesn't exist. For them, there is no such thing as soul, thoughts, feelings, beliefs, etc. They perceived these as nerve impulses flowing through our nerves. And if everything is material, then there's no need for a god."

"Wow. Do you plan to explain all this to me?"

"If we have enough time, I hope."

"Okay. What else drives young people away from faith?"

"The problem of evil."

"Which is?"

"If God is so good and beautiful, why does he allow evil to thrive and win in this world? Why do bad things happen to good people? Why do children die? etc."

"Yeah…that's a common one. I struggled with this for a while."

"See my point?"

"We're not equipped…"

"No we're not. There's also the diversity of religious paths and the arbitrariness of salvation. How do we choose the right path? If there's only one path and the rest are false, why doesn't God just guide us to that path? What responsibility does someone have if they're born to the wrong parents in the wrong tradition? And if all paths lead to salvation, then what's the point of following one path versus the other?"

"I see. These are important questions. Actually I myself wondered about this a lot before!"

"You must have. Most do. We just don't talk about these things."

"Man…" he said with a somber tone.

"Yep. Then there are modern moral objections to religious teachings, where people question certain injunctions and call them archaic and impractical, or even immoral and barbaric. Why does divine punishment need to be so harsh? What's the point of sending people to hell for eternity? How can stoning and flogging be okay? Why would a religion that claims to come from God allow men to have multiple wives, or take slaves? How come all religions breed violence and conflict? And other such arguments."

"These are all valid points though!"

"Didn't I tell you we are not prepared?"

"Oh God!"

"Last but not least is the exposure to ultra-liberal, postmodern ideals."

"Oh boy. I know where this is headed," he mumbled.

"I bet. Our generation now has to grapple with homosexuality and the LGBTQA+ movement as a reality. Our children are growing up surrounded by really kind and relatively amiable gay and transgender people, and others who subscribe to lifestyles antagonistic to religious teachings. So some people ask: what's the big deal about someone who just falls in love? Why is it wrong to love someone of the same gender? If this is how God created us, then how come it's a sin? If I feel in my heart like a girl, why should I refrain from being one? What harm did I cause anyone to rot in hell for it? Why is premarital sex religiously unacceptable if it's consensual? Why can't we all just get along and respect each other's choices? And the argument is: once religion and God are removed from the equation, harmony will finally settle."

"I can definitely see how many are influenced by these ideas… You're right. We are not prepared in any sense to handle this."

"Not only that we are not prepared. We don't even think this is a priority!"

"Why?" he asked curiously.

"Because for the longest time religious people were just busy with their esoteric theological arguments and endless juristic debates, feeling safe in our own bubbles, not knowing how fast the world is evolving -or devolving- around us."

"That's absolutely true. I don't know how many times folks in my mosque asked every single guest speaker that ever came to town the same set of questions they ask every time: is it halal to eat at McDonald's? Can I use a conventional mortgage to buy a house? And is it permissible to shake hands with the opposite gender?"

"As important as these questions might be to some, they're missing the bigger points: you have to believe in God first to acknowledge His law! Many people are steadily losing their grip over faith and are becoming gradually disenchanted," I said.

"True...But that's the thing. Believing in God will always just be a matter of faith. When science can answer most if not all of our questions, and when it's impossible to prove the concept of God, how can you make a strong argument for His existence without sounding superstitious and less intelligent?"

"Your question is the best manifestation of the terrible habits of thought that most of us have blindly accepted."

"How come?"

"The idea that science and technology can explain everything sounds like blind faith a lot more than the assumption that there are things, including objective truths, that can possibly lie beyond the realm of our senses. On what basis would atheists blame believers for accepting the notion of God "on faith" and without proof, when they themselves "believe," without any proof, that nothing exists that cannot be verified through science? That claim, in and of itself, has not been empirically proven. The scripture talks about the knowledge beyond the perception of man, or *ilm-al-Ghayb*. It's a requirement of faith to believe in the knowledge of the unseen. For some, this sounds superstitious, but for me, it sounds astoundingly objective and profoundly humble."

"How so?" he asked with great curiosity.

"Well, what the scripture compels us to do here is not to believe in superstitious powers and mythical fables, but rather, to accept the possibility that there exists knowledge beyond the realm of human discovery. That there's more to the world than what our senses can detect. Five hundred years ago, notions of flying across continents, or walking on the moon, would have been considered superstitious and foolish, and they rested on no scientific principles accepted at the time. Which long-held assumptions today will be completely debunked in due time? There's so much to be known and discovered. The fact that there are forces at play beyond the material is certain at best, and possible at least. It takes humility to acknowledge this, and a tremendous amount of hubris to reject it."

"I never really looked at it this way before. But here's my question: having doubts in the existence of God, and generating evidence to disprove His existence, are two different things. The first is possible, the second is not. Why does some doubt in God's existence cause some to simply lose faith? Why can't people at least be open to the possibility?"

"This is a very good question. You're absolutely right. Proving that God doesn't exist, is just as impossible as proving that He does. The statement "God doesn't exist" is an unfalsifiable claim, using the language of materialists. It makes me think sometimes: can someone really be a true atheist? I mean, when you think about it, atheists believe that God doesn't exist. Theists believe that God does exist. Both claims cannot be scientifically proven. They're both based in faith. And if the existence of God cannot be categorically ruled out, then there cannot be a true atheist really, right?"

"Wow! I guess. But what does this imply?"

"It implies that so-called atheism is an intellectual fallacy. One can either be a theist or an agnostic. It would make sense to say: well, I don't have any proof that God exists, but I cannot disprove it either. But to say: God doesn't exist, is more of a statement of faith than a statement of science or reason."

"If this is the case though, then why is atheism so pervasive? And why do many followers of faith fall in its traps?"

"Well, we probably have Aristotle to blame for this."

"Aristotle? The ancient Greek philosopher?"

"In the flesh."

"Does this have to do with philosophy being antagonistic to religion?"

"Philosophy is not antagonistic to religion. It diffuses faux beliefs only. In fact, the mindset in which philosophy and religion are incompatible may have exacerbated the inability of religious people to keep up with the changing times and actively combat fragile atheistic contentions."

"So when you say Aristotle you mean the historical figure and not what he represents?"

"Well, both actually!" I said with a smirk.

"Okay, are you going to tell me how, or do you want me to beg?"

"Alright. Let me start with a question: the assumption that once one has doubts in the existence of God he or she should give up faith, is a reflection of which wider social phenomenon?"

"I don't know..."

"It's a reflection of the widely accepted and rarely questioned binary logic: the black and white state of mind that governs the habits of thought of most modern human beings."

"What does this mean?"

"Think about it. We've always been taught that things are mutually exclusive. It's either you're happy or miserable, healthy or unhealthy, republican or democrat, conservative or liberal, pro-life or pro-abortion, gay or straight, and so forth. You can only be one or the other, the argument contends. People think that one state of existence is mutually exclusive to the other. I'm either in pain or bliss. I can either be skinny and healthy, or fat and unhealthy. Once this illness that I suffer from is gone, my quality of life will improve. If only I find a well-paying job, all my problems will go away. I cannot spend enough time with my kids right now because I need to work first and achieve financial independence. I don't volunteer in my community because I have to get through this phase at work. My marital life will improve once the kids are out at college. And the examples are too abundant to cite. Life for most of us is composed of mutually exclusive occurrences and events that are happening 'in-series', one phase is followed by the other, and so on. What happens in one phase needs to end first, before the next phase begins. This binary logic is so pervasive that it is seldom noticed anymore."

"It's absolutely true! This is how most people think. Is there another way though? Isn't this binary logic a true reflection of life?"

"If there isn't, I wouldn't have mentioned it, would I?" I said with a smirk.

"True…So what is the alternative way of thinking?"

"Well, that events in life unfold 'in-parallel' not 'in-series'. That the happenings of our world overlap and interlace and they certainly unfold with subtlety and graduality. That different states are not mutually exclusive. That the options are not binary, but abundant. There is no such thing as a pure state of pain or an unadulterated state of joy. There are some people who are skinny but still unhealthy, and others who manage to improve their marital lives before they become empty nesters, and some certainly manage to balance their time between family, work, community, and God while carrying heavy burdens upon weak shoulders. Day and night don't transition into each other abruptly. Your eyes have to experience both darkness and light simultaneously. You have to witness the milder days of spring as you transition from winter to summer, where both cold and warm intermingle. In the scriptures, the story of Moses is told. He got married, found a job, and built his family, while still searching for the truth. The Prophet Muhammad ﷺ managed to preserve the identity of his community, withstand the economic boycott, survive the humiliation of

Taaef, keep the migrants in Abyssinia positive, correspond with the Ansaar in Medina, all the while he was grieving for the loss of his wife and grandfather, only to go on and build a new community."

"Man! What a liberating perspective…" he said slowly, emphasising every word.

"It is, and you want to know why all this is relevant to the subject of atheism?"

"Yes!"

"Because this is why people lose their faith. Once they detect a seed of doubt in God's existence, they resort to a subconscious, but ever strong intellectual framework that most of us have involuntarily adopted: the dreaded binary logic that instructs us to choose sides. So they do, and in the process, they resolve the dichotomy by choosing one path at the expense of the other, thinking that they are mutually exclusive. If I have feelings towards the same gender, I must be gay and I need to 'come out'. I cannot believe in God and have doubts at the same time. Therefore if I have doubts, I need to forgo my belief in God. This is what happened to your nephew."

"So you're saying that my nephew lost his faith because he wasn't taught how to enable his faith to coexist with doubt?"

"Couldn't have put it more eloquently," I said with a smile.

"God - this is insane," he said with disbelief.

"I told you we are naked in this battle."

"Clearly. But what does this have to do with Aristotle?"

"Aristotelian philosophy, which ultimately emanated from the Greek religion, is still a dominant intellectual force in Western civilisation. Ancient Greek religion is based on the idea that gods and men are two separate entities, from two separate worlds, that are often at odds with each other. They cannot coexist and certainly cannot adapt to each other. In fact, in the ancient Greek religion, when man dies he doesn't go to heaven to be united with the gods. Rather, he or she goes into another heavenly realm to still be with man. This is the environment in which Aristotelian philosophy flourished. You sense the binary logic in all of Aristotle's writings and before him, Plato and Socrates. And this is the dichotomous, mutually exclusive thinking that we still suffer from to this day."

"Absolutely fascinating! But here's what puzzles me: the binary logic as you call it has existed for centuries. Why do we see the rise of atheism nowadays a lot more than before?"

"Two words: public schooling and social media."

"Schooling? But we've had schools for centuries!"

"I said schooling and social media. Both, together, are a recipe for disaster."

"How come?"

"Don't get me wrong. I'm not an opponent of the public school system. While I do hold very dearly the notion that it is a child's parents and his/her primary system of support that should be responsible for his/her education, I do understand, however, the value of the school system, especially in modern times. But here's the thing though: public schools are not designed for learning. They are more like centres for the dissemination of information. They 'prepare' not educate students."

"Prepare them for what?" he asked with a puzzled voice.

"For the workforce. Think of schools as platforms for job training and not beacons of knowledge and intellectual growth. They've become a place of socialising, acquiring bad habits, bullying, discarding talent, conformity, mixed up with some educational value, for the purpose of preparing children for the workforce."

"Didn't think you thought very little of the school system."

"It's more of a critique than anything. I still believe in its value, but not in total disconnect from a child's parents and his or her natural support system, in terms of extended family, religion, culture, mosque etc."

"So how does this lead to the rise of atheism?"

"Think about it. Kids spend most of their days under the care of complete strangers. Parents are busy, smartphones are rampant and social media has become the norm!"

"Sounds ominous, but I still can't make the connection."

"When parents are not very present in the picture, and when schools have disconnected kids from their culture, religion, family, support system, tradition and history, and in a complete lack of mentorship, where kids now rely on each other and the internet when they have questions, and when social media is so pervasive and keeps on providing false information and grants instant gratification, what do you think will happen to transcendental ideas such as God, morality etc?" I asked.

"Erode over time," he responded with hesitation.

"Precisely."

"Lord All-Mighty."

"I know."

"But aside from primary and secondary education, colleges and universities remain beacons of knowledge and objectivity right? One can trust their findings and conclusions at least," he asked earnestly.

"Perhaps, but with a grain of salt."

"Oh boy…Why?!"

"Because while you're right for the most part in your assessment of the institutions of higher education, you also need to understand that academic research is not always unbiased and disinterested."

"Really?"

"Yes. When research, in general, is determined and driven by government and private funding, how can it be entirely free of bias?"

"You're not suggesting that researchers would tamper their own evidence based on where the sources of funding are coming from, are you? At least the process is peer-reviewed."

"I'm not suggesting that. Remember I said that for the most part, the process is objective. Nonetheless, how do you explain the frequent publishing of conflicting 'studies'? One study suggests that a certain drug has a certain effect, and the other study suggests the opposite. Academic peers do review the process to ensure that it's systematic, but the room for bias still exists, because we do subjectively admit or discard data occasionally in order to reach certain conclusions. The pressure to publish mixed with the fear of losing funding is pretty powerful. But aside from that, large corporations are notorious for purchasing scientific research and shelving it because the end result would interfere with their market share or profit margins if such research saw the light. In other words, much of what is left in our hands is not necessarily the best or most valid ideas, rather, what men in power allowed us to have."

"You are a total skeptic."

"I take that as a compliment," I said with a smile.

"But here's another question. When my nephew keeps referring to science as the most reliable tool to discovering the truth, and when he keeps using the lack of scientific evidence for God, wouldn't any attempt to undermine science and the value of academic research appear like a desperate attack on objective truth as opposed to generating counter-arguments and engaging in honest dialogue?"

"Who said anything about undermining science and academic research? I was just saying they have to occasionally be taken with a grain of salt. Even scientists don't have the audacity to claim they have answers to all questions or that their process is free of bias and human error."

"So science still has a great utility, right?"

"Without a doubt."

"So, is it possible to use science to prove the existence of God? Isn't the scripture filled with strong statements about science, biology, etymology etc? If we can generate strong scientific arguments from divine revelation, wouldn't that be the best counter to atheistic ideas as we fight back using their tools?"

"No. It would be a terrible idea."

"Why?" he asked in shock.

"Many have attempted to wrap their heads around the ever-illusive "scientific marvels of the scriptures" and every attempt fell flat on its face."

"How come?"

"Well, because they forgot, or perhaps ignored the simple fact that science is a volatile institution. It evolves and changes. New research renders old ideas obsolete. Today's accepted scientific norms are tomorrow's relics. How many assumptions about science and the world were deemed unfit at some point when new ideas were generated and new discoveries were made?"

"Many."

"Which brings me to my point: associating the timeless spiritual truths of the scripture with the wavering paradigms of science is not only futile, but it's also actually very precarious."

"Does the same apply to philosophy?"

"In what sense?"

"I mean is it just as bad an idea to use philosophical arguments to validate or invalidate religion?"

"Philosophy is an institution of thought that verifies and corroborates claims about the world using reason and rationality. While it certainly occupies a more intimate place vis-a-vis religion than science, it would be erroneous to assume that it rests on a higher intellectual ground than religious thought. Philosophy can judge whether ideas are logical or not, but it is not without error."

"How can a process of reason and logic be erroneous?"

"Our logic occasionally fails us. At the end of the day, what's 'logical' is still bound by what we know, and perhaps what we see and experience. For a frog at the bottom of a pit, it's perfectly 'logical' to assume the non-existence of mountains, but is it true? Philosophy, just like science, cannot explain human feelings, self-consciousness, or the desire to follow moral standards. Plato argued that the most just society is governed by "guardians" who are conceived as children through eugenics, which is a meticulously orchestrated breeding process to maximise the best traits of the genetic pool. I'm sure this sounded logical to Plato and the philosophers who celebrated Eutopia for centuries, but in today's terms it's not only illogical, it's criminal."

"Wow! So what is the place of science and philosophy then

within the conversation about God and the world? If they cannot judge the validity of religion, then how can they be used?"

"By applying their methodologies to eliminate the false positives!" I responded.

"Oh boy - big words again!"

"No big words here. Do you know the difference between false positives, true positives, false negatives, and true negatives?"

"Umm - no..!"

"No worries. Let me explain. They're logical tools to verify claims and characterise them. For example, let's assume that there is a claim that has to do with whether a woman is pregnant. How can we corroborate or invalidate the claim?"

"By taking a pregnancy test?"

"Precisely. If the test is positive, and she turns out to be pregnant, then we'd say we have a true positive. But if the test is positive, but it turns out that she's not pregnant, then what would we say then?"

"Man…this is like math."

"Trust me. It's not that hard. Think about it."

"We'd say that we have a false positive?" he said with hesitation after a brief pause.

"Exactly! You're getting the hang of it."

"I think I get it. So if she tests negative but is actually pregnant, then we'd have a false negative?"

"Yes! And what would be the last possibility?"

"That she tests negative, and is not actually pregnant, in which case we'd have a true negative, right?"

"There you go! Now tell me, how do we apply this useful logical utility to religion?" I asked.

"I have no idea…" he said with a puzzled tone.

"Come on!" I cried.

"Seriously …. I don't know. How is this related to the usefulness of science and philosophy?"

"As I said before, by applying them only to eliminate the false positives."

"You mean in terms of what?"

"In terms of claims of religious truths."

"How?"

"It's simple. As a matter of principle, science and philosophy should not be applied to verify whether a religious claim is valid. Even if we verify that certain claims of one religion or another are valid, It doesn't mean that the entire framework of that religion is valid. it could still be man-made. Many human thought constructs might be valid, but it doesn't mean they're divine. Rather, we apply the tools of science and philosophy to exclude the claims that pretend to be true but are actually false."

"How do we do that?"

"Remember the pregnant woman example? If a certain religion claims to be the truth, but a major tenet of its articles of faith or its ritual practices contradicts science or logic, then we have ourselves what?"

"A false positive?"

"Exactly."

"Can you give me an example?"

"Well, if the creed of a certain religion argues that man and dinosaur walked the earth 3000 years ago when this runs contrary to the simple fundamentals of science, natural history, and carbon dating, it would be easy to dismiss it. Or if a religion claims fidelity to multiple gods, going against the basic notions of reason making it clear that if God is infinite then there has to be only one God, it's easy to dismiss that religion's claim to truthfulness as a false positive, and so on."

"What is the end goal of this mental exercise though?"

"To minimise the number of options left on your table of spiritual consideration to hopefully just one!"

"And that would be the true positive?"

"There you go!"

"What if there is more than one left?"

"That's when I say the Creator will have to interfere to guide you to His one true path through intuition and divine guidance. It requires lots of prayers and earnest appeals to God."

"Intuition? But isn't that kind of superstitious?"

"Denying that there are realms of objective knowledge beyond human perception is what's superstitious! Remember, I only said that relying on intuition, or as mystic theologians called it *Ilhaam*, becomes only valid after you've eliminated other possible choices through science and reason. In other words, what I'm saying is that finding the true positive is a mere gift from God reserved to those who have sincerely laboured to attain it."

"Man…this is mind-blowing.."

"In a good way, I hope," I said.

"Okay. I can definitely see how science and philosophy have their limitations with regard to deciding which organised path to God to follow. However, do they have any utility in actually 'proving' that God exists?"

It was now my turn to ask. "Can you elaborate on your question?"

"What I'm asking here is simple: what other instruments do we have at our disposal to respond to atheists unless it's a language they can understand? iIf they use science or philosophy to disqualify God, can we use them to qualify Him?"

"Philosophers have been doing this for thousands of years!" I said.

"Seriously? Philosophers used reason and logic to prove the existence of God?" he asked.

"Absolutely! For thousands of years those arguments were perpetuated to make a case for God, and to this day, none of this has been completely refuted," I responded.

"This is incredible! Can you share the arguments with me?" he asked.

"Umm…I promised the phone call was going to be short and here you are dragging me on for more than two hours. Can we do this later?"

"Oh! Yes…sorry."

"Do you feel better about your nephew?"

"Of course. At least there is a glimpse of hope that I can do something to help him."

"Great. Let's touch base soon."

"Let's do that. Thanks!"

"You're welcome."

## Chapter 2

# Design

"Imam, I hope you have time to follow up on our last conversation!" he said after a community breakfast on a pleasant morning.

"Sure. Which conversation?"

"The one about my nephew losing his faith and the existence of God."

"Ah yes! Of course. That's an unfinished conversation."

"Let's finish it then."

"By all means. Walk with me," I said while I made my way to my office.

"Let me ask you first. How do you feel?" I asked.

"About what?"

"About this whole thing? I mean, are you still mad at your nephew?"

"In a way, yes. A little. After all, he put his family through a lot."

"Remember what we said. We have failed this generation in two ways: first, we have not provided them with the necessary tools that can help them as they grapple with the stomach-churning realities of the new atheistic religion. And to add insult to injury, we have failed to grant them access to the proper channels by which they can communicate with us their spiritual and intellectual ailments. We don't listen, and when we do, we get angry and upset, blocking all doorways for positive encounters with our children and their generation about the truths of faith and the realities of God."

"Agreed. This is why I'm not that angry anymore," he said.

"Let's be productive. Where did we leave off last time?" I asked.

"The false positives and true positives!"

"And then how did we end the conversation?"

"You said that there are philosophical approaches to establish the existence of God that we all need to know."

"Let's talk about that today."

"I'm all ears!" he said with excitement.

"Let me mention one thing first. Belief in God seems like the natural state of the self. Crying out for that power beyond the universe, seeking His help, feeling His presence, is how each and every one of us is programmed. Rejecting God and envisioning a universe without Him requires effort. Many atheists always play the prove-to-me-that-God-exists card. My response to this is simple: prove to me that He doesn't! The natural disposition of all hearts is to accept God. The burden of proof should not be on the believers."

"Yet, you're willing to sit down with me and engage in lengthy conversations about God?"

"Yes, and I would without hesitation. I just wanted to point out to you that acceptance of God seems natural, while the rejection of God seems artificial. There seems to be a significant amount of self-absorption and outright hubris that govern the thought process of many prophets of modern-day atheism. There is no amount of logic or philosophising that can cure that. Our counter-message should be directed to the bewildered, not the obstinate. I will engage people of faith who struggle any day or even confused seekers of the truth. But I have no interest in debating atheists who have lost the desire to listen."

"But it is also true that many atheists are just honest people who have failed to find God. They're not arrogant or angry. Some of them might even be depressed that they lost the presence of God. Isn't this also true?"

"I have to concede to this. But humble atheists who gradually lost their faith, suffer silently and are way too busy with their own journey to write books, give lectures and fill discussion boards and social media with mockery of the believers. This type of atheist is never the target of my critique. It's just the obnoxious type," I said with a suppressed chuckle.

"Fair enough. Let's start then," he said enthusiastically.

"One of the earliest, simplest, and most effective arguments for God was originally propagated by Thomas Aquinas in the 13th century and was later detailed and refined by William Paley of the 18th century. The name it was given over the centuries is "The Design Argument". It was also supported by philosophers such as Rene Descartes and physicists such as Isaac Newton."

"What is the main premise of the Design Argument?" he asked with excessive attention.

"In a nutshell, the Design Argument states that the meticulous order of the universe, its consistency, and precise design cannot be the work of random chance. It's simply too complex to be arbitrary. There's both purpose and order in the universe, pointing to a Maker," I said.

"Interesting. How does the universe having a purpose lead to the conclusion that there is a Maker?"

"Paley uses the watchmaker analogy to explain this. Imagine for a second that you found a watch in the desert. What will you automatically assume?"

"That it fell off someone's wrist?"

"Yes. But you will also assume that someone made it, right?"

"Of course."

"Since there is a watch, there has to be a watchmaker. The watch is a complex device with lots of moving parts, and its purpose is to tell the time. This analogy can be applied to the universe. It's very complex, filled with moving parts, and it seems consistent in its design. The universe is far more complex than a watch. In fact, the human eye is more complex than a watch! It has more than 2 million moving parts all working in unison. It processes more than 36,000 bits of data every hour, all for the purpose of allowing us to see the environment around us. In fact, the retina relays data to the brain at the speed of about 10 mbps, which is comparable to broadband internet speed."

"How astounding!" he said with amazement.

"And if you think the human eye is complicated, consider this: the human body is made of about 37 trillion cells! And if that figure is astounding, check this out: there are over 100 trillion good bacteria in the human body, three times more than the actual number of cells! Which means we're mainly composed of bacteria! Of course bacteria is much smaller than human cells, but the point still stands. This complex arrangement has the purpose of maintaining human life and survival. Bacteria work harmoniously with each other and with our cells to basically keep us alive. And this is just us. This duo of complexity and purpose can be argued about almost everything in the universe. And if the universe is complex and purposeful, then it must have a maker!"

"Sounds simple enough. What about order?" he asked.

"Well, the universe is fine-tuned with very consistent laws that contribute directly to the sustaining of life. Everything is regulated with strict rules of physics. You find those fundamental constants, or what they call cosmic singularities, everywhere we look around us. The acceleration of gravity(g), the speed of light in vacuum(c), the Gravitational constant(G), are but a few examples. In fact, there are a total of 19 constants in physics. These are mathematical values that we just discovered. It just seems like these values have been pre-determined by a force beyond physics."

"I've studied all this in my physics classes, but never looked at it this way! It's true. Why is g=9.8 m/s2 instead of any other value? That is fascinating!"

"For sure. Moreover, order is manifested in so many other aspects of the universe. Take, for example, the balance between matter and antimatter. It's accurate to one part in ten billion. If it was any more or any less, the universe wouldn't have ever come to existence!"

"Amazing!"

"Physicists even contend that the universe wouldn't have arisen had the rate of the Big Bang expansion been one billionth of a percent faster or slower!"

"This is profound. So it's mathematically impossible that the universe's complexity is just mere probability?" he asked.

"Well, the probability of the random formulation of one enzyme of amino acids in a protein strand within the human body is 1 in 1020. Since the human body has 2000 enzymes, the probability rises to 1 in 1040,000. And keeping in mind that enzyme formulation is one of many complex processes of life, including DNA, RNA, cells, molecules, organs, etc, the probability approaches 1 to infinity!" I answered.

"I can see how impossible this can be. But here's my question. Some will say given enough time, any unlikely probability will eventually become possible. Isn't that true?"

"It is, provided that that period of time is shorter than the actual life of the universe, right?"

"Not sure if I'm following you."

"What I mean is this: if I say that it's very improbable for someone to be hit by a meteor, someone might say yes it's improbable, but it's still possible, given enough time. The response would be yes, but this time has to be shorter than someone's life span. So if it would take 200 years for the statistical probability of a meteor hitting someone to actually occur, it becomes virtually impossible considering that no one lives that long."

"Oh! I see what you're saying. So even if complexity is possible through random chance, it would take longer than the life of the universe itself for this to happen, which makes it impossible, right?"

"Yes. It's true that the improbable will become probable given enough time, but that time has to be shorter than the lifetime of the object that is subject to that probability. Otherwise, it becomes not only improbable but impossible."

"I think I understand this point, but has it been statistically proven that such probabilities would take longer than the lifetime of the universe itself?"

"Indeed. Let's take a protein molecule as an example. On average a protein molecule is composed of about 150 amino acids. For this number of amino acids to "self-assemble" perchance into a fully functional protein molecule, it would statistically take about 3.15 x 10115 years for this to happen. So is it possible? Yes, given the passage of enough time. But can the age of our universe support this?"

"Of course not. The universe is only 13.7 x 109 years old, which is astronomically less."

"Exactly. To demonstrate this point further, James F. Coppedge in his popular book 'Evolution: Possible or Impossible', draws out a thought experiment in which an amoeba is to traverse the universe at the speed of one foot a year, crossing the 90 billion light-years that is the diameter of the observable universe, carrying on its back one atom each time. How much time would it take to transport the entire universe from one place to another?"

"One atom at a time?" he asked with a horrified voice.

"Yes, one atom at a time."

"It would take an untold number of years of course!"

"Using 90 billion light-years as the assumed diameter of the observable universe, it would take the amoeba, traveling one foot per year, 5.7 x 1027 years to travel across the universe, drop the atom off, and return for more. Since there are approximately 1080 atoms in the universe, the amoeba could transport them all in 5.7 x 10107 years at the rate of one atom per round trip."

"This is simply unthinkable! But what's the point here?"

"You know how many round trips this amoeba needs to make in order for the protein molecule I talked about earlier to self-assemble?"

"How many?" he asked with anticipation.

"The amoeba would have plenty of time, traveling just one foot per year, carrying one atom per round trip, to haul over 56 million universes before one protein molecule is formed by random chance."

"I have nothing to say. This is simply unfathomable to me!"

"Understandably. And this doesn't take into consideration other protein molecules working together in unison, or more complex biological processes, or the construction of billions of cells, other living organisms, planets, galaxies etc. Random chance might be mathematically plausible but the universe simply hasn't been around long enough in order for that chance to be possible. The point is that keeping these mathematical improbabilities in mind, it's inevitable to conclude that the universe, with its complex design and meticulous formulations, had an initiator that willed for it to be a certain way, and that it cannot be the product of mere random chance."

"Wow! How can anyone still be an atheist after hearing this?"

"Trust me, some still do."

"How?" he cried.

"Well, 18th-century philosopher David Hume argues vigorously against the Design Argument, contending that the universe is in fact not orderly, because of the collision of galaxies, supernovas, cosmic radiation, meteor impacts, volcanoes, cyclones etc."

"And how do we respond to that?"

"Well, that the collision of galaxies, the eruption of earthquakes or the ripping of tornadoes, are all-natural phenomena that are in and of themselves still reflective of physical laws that are very precise, in terms of motion, energy, electromagnetic fields etc. In fact, all of these catastrophic events represent tremendous balance, in which the universe restores equilibrium based on its predetermined laws."

"So seemingly disorderly or catastrophic events are still in line with the order of the universe?"

"Fundamentally, yes."

"Makes sense. Is this all the critique of the Design perspective?" he asked curiously.

"No. Hume also argues that even if the Design Argument is valid, it doesn't necessarily lead to the conclusion that there's only one God, or whether that God is infinite or not, or if it's actually God, or just a designer or an architect, or whether God is good or not."

"And how do we respond to this?"

"That the Design Argument doesn't aspire to answer all these questions. It simply establishes that a designer, with the qualifications of God, exists, that's it. Other philosophical arguments can address the rest of the inquiries."

"Fair enough. But if we assume that there is order and purpose in the universe, why does this lead directly to the assumption that God exists? Is it possible that the universe is just orderly and purposeful on its own?"

"This is what naturalists obviously argue, but no, it's not possible."

"Why not?"

"Because once you establish order and purpose, the natural questions would be: how do you explain them? How can a non-living mechanical order such as that of the universe decide for itself to be so purposeful? And what's the point of purpose if it doesn't have a designer?"

"I see. I do have an important question, though."

"What is it?"

"If we accept that the universe has both order and purpose and that this implies a designer, you know that this begs a predictable question, right?"

"Of course. They'll ask: who designed the designer?"

"You've been doing this for so long it seems."

"Oh yeah. I've seen it all."

"Okay. So how do we respond to that?"

"By saying that asking the predictable question: who designed the designer, leads to an infinite regress, is a logical fallacy. If we establish that the universe has a purpose and that it must have a designer, we would settle for this answer, because if we don't, we'll have to start asking questions about who designed the designer, and who designed the previous designer, and so on, and this will inevitably lead us into the fallacy of an infinite number of events that need to have happened before the current event occurs."

"And what's wrong with this?"

"That it's impossible for infinity to have already happened. Infinity is an abstraction in the human mind. It's useful for mathematical equations but doesn't exist in the physical world. If it did, then an infinite number of events must precede us first, which is impossible. It's just like trying to jump out of a bottomless pit. You don't have ground under you to take a leap. If an infinite number of events is required before our current reality occurs, then we should have never existed. If the current event, which is the universe as we know it, is contingent upon events that have not happened yet, or impossible to happen, then this current event shouldn't have happened in the first place, and we shouldn't have existed. This is the fallacy of asking the question: what caused the original cause?"

He paused while shaking his head in disbelief.

"God All-Mighty…. my mind is blown…But how do we get out of this fallacy then?" he asked.

"By settling for the notion that the designer is un-designed. And if the designer is not designed, then the designer has to be God, because only God can bring Himself to existence. Everything else is contingent, meaning it depends its being and existence on something, or someone else. The Creator doesn't exist within the physical universe, and therefore is not subject to its limitations. He's not contingent and certainly is un-caused, because the universe as a contingency, is impossible to have just caused itself."

"Absolutely brilliant!"

"There's one more thing I want to add here though. Even though the Design Argument doesn't directly make claims about God being infinite or good, my mind is perfectly comfortable with both assumptions being true."

"How come?"

"Think about it. Everything in our universe is material, finite and contingent. Since we just established that the Designer is un-caused, immaterial, and is not subject to the limitations of the universe, then He has to be infinite."

"How did you come to this conclusion?"

"Because any finite entity that could have presumably caused the universe, even alien life, is still bound by material limitations, and can still possibly be a part of 'another' universe, and therefore would still be contingent. The only way 'The Designer' can be in-contingent is to be infinite."

"What if they say the universe was caused by multiple gods?"

"This too would be impossible."

"Why?"

"Logically speaking, if I said, hypothetically, that this table is infinite, what does that imply?"

"Not sure."

"It implies that it's the only table there is."

"How?"

"Because if a table is infinite, then there's no room for other tables to exist. This infinite table occupies every possible space that other tables would have occupied."

"I can see that."

"With the same token, if I said God is infinite, then there has to be one God. Only in a finite existence can you have multiplicity."

"Multiplicity?"

"Meaning multiples of one object. Many gods in this case."

"I see. This is truly fascinating. I'm so grateful for this conversation."

"It's my pleasure. Anytime."

"If this is just the first argument for God, I'm dying to learn about the rest!"

"Let's touch base soon, inshaAllah."

"Thank you!"

"You're welcome! By the way, can I ask you to do me a favor?" I asked.

"By all means!"

I grabbed a brown keychain from my pocket, with the word

*Hikmah*, Arabic for wisdom, engraved on it.

"Will you please give this to your nephew as a gift from me?"
I asked.

"Of course. Do you think he'll accept it?" he asked.

"I think so."

"What's the significance of the keychain?"

"This is a keychain that my teacher gave me during the early
days of my knowledge pursuit. I just want your nephew to feel
that we're both passengers on this journey together, pursuing and
seeking the same thing: a wisdom that embodies the truth."

"I will make sure he gets the gift. Thank you."

"You're welcome!"

## Chapter 3

# Cause

"Assalamu alaykum wa rahmatullah…. Assalamu alaykum wa rahmatullah," I said as I concluded the congregational prayer, after which I sat silently in the *Mihrab*, doing my supplications, filling my eyes with the beautiful calligraphy of the mosque's *mihrab* (prayer niche). It was my habit to eventually turn around and face the congregants as they finalise their prayers as well. This time, a tap on my shoulder startled me. I looked to the person who was standing right behind me. It was him, the uncle. He looked at me with eyes filled with both apology and hope, and said in jubilation "Imam! My nephew made contact today!"

"Assalamu alaykum brother!" I said with a smile.

"Wa alaykum assalam! I'm so sorry to interrupt your supplications."

"Please don't worry about it. Sit right here next to me," I said, as I gestured to the *Mihrab*.

"Sit here with you?" he asked in disbelief.

"Of course! Please." He sat down reluctantly and looked at me with a nervous smile.

"So you said your nephew made contact?" I asked.

"Yes, he did!"

"Alhamdulillah! How's he?" I asked.

"Seems in a better state. Asked about me and the family and suggested that we have lunch together soon."

"Great! When do you plan to meet?"

"Well, I need to learn how to debate him first before I meet!"

he said with a serious face.

"What do you mean?"

"I have to be able to argue with him and possibly diffuse his claims when I see him. What's the point of meeting him before I learn more about atheism?"

"The point is that he's your nephew! There needs to be no reason or cause for meeting him," I said.

"So walk into the battlefield unarmed?"

"What battlefield?" I said loudly, after which I realised that the echo from the *mihrab* (prayer niche) carried my words around the mosque, and other worshippers raised their heads and looked at me with intrigue.

"Have you ever considered that perhaps this over-dramatic attitude is what pushed your nephew away in the first place?" I whispered sarcastically.

"Imam, please don't joke about this. I already feel horrible as it is."

"I don't mean to make fun of you. All I'm saying is that you're his uncle. You don't have to find answers, or build arguments or weave philosophical contentions in order to show him your love. Sometimes expressing genuine emotion can go much farther than calculated intellectualism."

"So, what should we talk about if we meet?"

"Well, what did you talk about before?"

"I don't know...family stuff, school, life, all that."

"Why not talk about the same thing now?"

"So make small talk, and ignore the fact that he walked away from his family's faith and tradition?" he asked with an angry tone.

"Good things happen to those who are patient. In this initial phase after he made contact, he needs to feel comfortable that he can talk to you without judgement. He reached out for one of two reasons. Either he's still struggling and has many questions and needs someone to talk to, or that he wants to normalise relations and seek acceptance from the family for what he chose to do. Either way, questions about the path he took will come up, and that's when you naturally interject with your own thoughts."

"So, wait until he brings things up before I address them?" he asked with hesitation.

"Yes! Surprise him by not addressing the elephant in the room. Use reverse psychology and let him bring it up and ask questions, in which case your responses will be perfectly natural without any imposition," I answered.

"Ah, man...I'm so not cut out for this," he said as he rolled his eyes and looked the other way.

"None of us really are. No one is prepared for this upheaval like I said before. We just have to do what we can and leave the rest in the hands of God," I said assuredly.

"Amen...So should we go back to the atheism discussion?"

"Yes! Where did we stop last time?"

"We covered the first argument for God, which is the Design Argument."

"Great. Let's talk about another very popular argument for God."

"I'm excited already"

"You're beginning to like this stuff huh?"

"Oh yeah! It's so intellectually liberating."

"Happy to hear. So this particular argument for God is called 'The Cosmological First Cause' argument."

"Sounds loaded."

"Maybe, but it's really powerful."

"So who came up with this argument?" he asked.

"It was Aristotle at first, and then modified by Saint Thomas Aquinas in later centuries."

"Fascinating! What does it say?"

"Simply put, God is the "Unmoved Mover," or the "Prime Mover" of the universe, who causes everything but is NOT in and Himself subject to any causality. He's the axle, and all the other parts of the wheel, tire, frame, brakes etc. move except Him."

"So if God is the Prime Cause, then He Himself doesn't have

a cause, right?"

"Exactly. Observing the universe leads to a solid conclusion: that everything is caused, or using a fancy philosophical term, contingent. Every object is dependent in its origin and sustaining on something else. And if that's the case, then the primary cause of everything has to be uncaused Himself, because He's immaterial and transcendental."

"Sounds simple and elegant."

"It's one of the earliest arguments for God. And was perpetuated throughout the centuries."

"How can they refute this then?"

"Well, they try. David Hume, again, rejects the idea of causation and argues that the search for a cause is a product of the human mind and based in the human experience. The universe, for Hume, cannot be experienced, therefore it is not necessarily caused."

"But that doesn't make sense," he said with loud dismay.

"Lower your voice!" I said with a muffled laugh.

"Sorry!" he whispered.

"Bertrand Russell, following in Hume's footsteps, argues that the universe is just there, and that's all. There's no cause and there's no purpose."

"This irks me."

"It shouldn't. We must always be open to honest inquiry and tough questions. My simple response to both Hume and Russell is that their assumption that the universe cannot be experienced, therefore should not be assumed to have had a cause like the objects we experience regularly, is false. The universe IS experienced every day through those objects because they are made of the same stuff. I don't need to travel to the edge of the universe to experience it. It's made of the same components the earth is made of, therefore I experience it every day."

"Shouldn't that kill the atheistic perspective right then and there?"

"Well, it doesn't. Some acknowledge that the universe is perhaps made of parts that are contingent. But they argue that it is a logical fallacy to assume that just because the parts have a certain property that the whole also has that property. After all, saying all the bricks that make a wall are small, doesn't imply that the wall is small."

"But that's not what we're saying! We're not saying the wall is small, rather that the wall is made of dirt, just like the bricks!"

"Atheists would say some generalisations work and some don't, and the universe belongs to the ones that don't."

"On what basis?"

"Not clear to me, except of course to keep their arguments consistent."

"This is just remarkable," he said with astonishment.

"I agree. But you have to have the patience to follow their arguments, their lines of thought, and dismantle them logically, one by one."

"Agreed. I'm hungry for more! What other arguments for God do we need to discuss?"

"The most famous of all: The Kalam Cosmological argument!"

"Kalam?"

"Yes, Kalam - as in the medieval Muslim scholastic tradition."

"What's the scholastic tradition?"

"It's the tradition of theologians who use intellectual and rational arguments to establish the existence of God. So unlike philosophy, inquiry starts with the assumption that God exists and proceeds to prove that. Kalam was the Muslim version of that intellectual process."

"Fascinating. Does that mean the origin of that argument came from Muslim thinkers?" he inquired with excitement.

"Indeed. It was initially articulated by the great medieval theologian and philosopher Ghazali and later cited by other philosophers such as al-Farabi and iIbn-Rushd. It hinges upon the same premises of other cosmological arguments, with a specific variation."

"So what does it say?"

"It goes like this. 1: Anything that has a beginning, has a cause for its beginning. 2: The universe has a beginning. 3: Therefore, the universe has a cause for its beginning. 4: And since science cannot provide us with an explanation as to what that cause could be through physical laws, then the cause must be personal, meaning a person, and not some mechanical process, and this personal cause is what we call God."

"Pretty straightforward to me. But I can see some possible refutations."

"Like what?"

"Like, for instance, the assumption that the universe has a beginning."

"How can that be refuted?" I asked.

"Well, someone might say why do you assume the universe is finite? What if it's infinite?"

"Remember what we said about an infinite regress of causes? If the universe has been around for infinity, then an infinite number of events must have already taken place in order for us to arrive at the current point of time in the continuum. And since it's impossible that an infinite number of events have already occurred, then the universe must be finite."

"But why is it impossible for an infinite number of events to have happened before we arrive at the current event?"

"Because it's similar to trying to jump out of a bottomless pit as we said before. You need ground to take the leap. You need a beginning for the following event to happen. If the current event, as in this moment right now, is preceded by another event, then that preceding event is a precursor to the current moment. Right?"

"Yes."

"And the event before was preceded by another event that is ultimately its precursor, right?"

"Sure."

"So if we keep going back, every event must be preceded by another event in order for it to take place, right?"

"Right."

"That's what infinite regress is. It's impossible for an infinite number of events to have already happened. Infinity, by its very definition, will keep going back forever. So there's no starting point, for the next event, and the next event, and the next event, etc. till the current event, to have taken place."

"I think I understand it now."

"Great. So if an infinite regress is impossible, then what?" I asked, making sure he understood.

"Then there must have been a starting point for the universe."

"Or its creation as people of faith would say. Science also proved beyond doubt that the universe has a beginning, at the consternation of many scientists and philosophers including Einstein. It would have been convenient if the universe had been beginningless. After all, if it's always been around, then who needs God?"

"This is super powerful. What kind of refutations are given to this argument?"

"They say even if our universe is finite, there could be an infinite number of parallel universes out there, and that would cause the Kalam argument to fall flat on its face."

"Parallel universes? How can that even be proven?" he inquired.

"It can't. In fact, there is no possible methodology of scientific research, today or in the future, that can allow us to take a peek beyond the universe and see what actually lies there. The theory is entirely unfalsifiable."

"What is unfalsifiable?"

"It means it cannot be tested to be proven right or wrong. It's mere conjecture."

"Got it. But if it's not falsifiable, how can scientists still believe in its validity?"

"It's exactly what you said. Believe. That's what many scientists do. Many atheists are often critical of people of faith for "believing" in the unfalsifiable premise of a higher power while allowing themselves to also "believe" in the unfalsifiable premise of parallel universes."

"Remarkable."

"Indeed. But even if the theory of parallel universes is valid, it still can't save the refutations to the Kalam argument. After all, even if there's an infinite number of universes out there, who brought them to being? And it cannot be an infinite regress of causes either. One way or the other they have to come back to the same roadblock: who caused the initial event?"

"Unless, of course, they reject the premise that events need a cause in the first place!" he said with a nervous laugh.

I chuckled.

"Wait…someone actually thinks stuff can happen without a cause?" he asked with disbelief.

"Oh yeah. Didn't I tell you we're so not prepared?"

"Unbelievable …This is what our kids are exposed to on a daily basis?"

"And more. Trust me. It's a detracted battle and we better be prepared."

"So how can something happen without a cause?"

"They argue sometimes that the premise of causation itself has not been scientifically proven. To which we say perhaps, but it is based on an empirical generalisation derived from our daily encounters and scientific experiences. The premise of causation is more or less a metaphysical intuition that simply cannot be denied by any serious person."

"I can't believe that we have to discuss this," he said while shaking his head.

"We absolutely do. Others may accept causality at the level of conventional physics, but they say in quantum physics, events happen all the time without proper cause."

"Oh boy. I know nothing about quantum physics"

"Most people don't. Let me simplify it for you. Objects in their macro sense, meaning objects that can be palpable through the senses, are subject to the laws of physics, expounded by Newton,

Einstein, and other physicists, therefore have a clear cause for any change that occurs in or to them. But at their molecular level, these laws of physics don't apply. The behaviour of molecules is not predictable. Particles do not follow the same laws of physics that can explain the physical world, and that includes causation. So some atheists argue that while causation may play a role in ordinary objects, it plays no role at the quantum level, therefore, events can happen without a cause, including the bringing to existence of the universe."

"This is so complicated, but I think I get the gist of it."

"Glad to hear, but even then, they're still wrong."

"How?"

"Because they confuse unpredictability with lack of causality," I said.

"How?"

"Without going into the nitty-gritty of quantum physics, the behaviour of quantum particles might be impossible to predict, but it doesn't mean it doesn't have a cause."

"So regardless of how you look at things, we can all agree that every contingent object, the universe included, has a cause, right?" he asked.

"Right," I answered.

"But how is a discussion on quantum physics even relevant to the creation of the universe?"

"Because the beginning of the universe was a quantum event."

"Oh yeah - sorry - The Big Bang! The explosion of the first particle!" he said excitedly.

"Precisely. This is why we have to take the quantum argument seriously. Famed physicist Heisenberg proved that quantum behaviour is contingent upon the observer, meaning, a particle will behave differently depending on who's observing and when and where, without any intervention from the observer. This led physicists to believe that the behaviour of a particle cannot be predicted. This is called indeterminacy. But it still doesn't preclude the fact that even though the behaviour of a quantum particle cannot be predicted, it still has a cause."

"This is still a little obscure to me, but it sounds satisfactory. Here's a question though: what if they say the universe may be caused, but perhaps it was caused by aliens or another force beyond our perception, and not necessarily God?"

"Not entirely impossible logically, but it makes no difference, because we'd ask: who caused the cause? Who brought the aliens to existence?"

"Oh! So even if it's created by aliens, then we'd ask: who created the aliens?"

"In a finite regress type of sense obviously. There ultimately has to be a cause that is not bound by the same physical laws."

"So what are the qualities of that cause?"

"Well, if our logic still holds water, we can infer that the 'original' cause possesses the following qualities: first, uncaused, since He is the original cause. Second, immaterial, since He doesn't belong to this universe and its physical reality, therefore cannot be bound by its material limitations. Lastly, timeless, since He doesn't exist within the space-time continuum, which is a quality of this universe."

"My heart is at great ease," he said with relief.

"Glad to hear that," I said with gratitude.

"Hey, by the way, I gave my nephew your *Hikmah* keychain. He took it from me, looked at it, and put it in his pocket without saying a word," he said with a curious smile.

"Alhamdulillah."

"In all honesty though, I can't get enough of this! Can you share with me other arguments for God?"

"Sure. We still have a ways to go. But can we do this some other time? Promised my kids to spend the rest of the day with them!"

"Oh fine," he said with a big smile. "See you soon, inshaAllah!"

"Stay sane!"

"I will!"

By the time he left, I realised we were the last in the mosque. I took a quick glance at the beautiful calligraphy ornamenting the soffit. My eyes caught the Quranic verse, "Indeed, only those of knowledge are in awe of God".[1] I turned around to face the inside of the *mihrab* (prayer niche) again, and made sure to close my eyes, feeling enveloped by the endless grace and presence of God, and prayed silently.

*Chapter 4*

# Ontology

It was a pleasant gathering. A dear friend's son was graduating high school. 4.4 GPA, Stanford scholarship, he was the pride of his family. But he was my personal pride as well. This kid had been a student of mine since he came to Sunday school at the age of five. Insightful, disciplined, and deeply pious, qualities you seldom see in a young man these days. We were at a dinner gathering to celebrate his success with him and his family. At dinner time, I made myself a plate and sat in the corner to have a bite.

Then I saw him. The uncle with whom I had been having conversations about God seemed to have been invited to the same event. He was sitting by himself in the backyard caught in his own thoughts. I took my plate, walked out to the backyard, and approached him gently.

"It's not Ramadan you know," I said with a smile.

"Oh Imam! Good to see you. How have you been?"

"Not too bad. You?"

"Grateful to God for everything."

"Why are you sitting here by yourself while the rest of us are having dinner? You're not fasting are you?" I said with a smile.

"No. Just consumed by my own thoughts."

"What kind of thoughts?"

"God, the universe, my nephew. You know - the usual," he said with a sigh. "Can't get my mind off everything you discussed with me."

"Are these conversations helping you solidify your perception of and devotion to God? Because for me that's the most important question. These conversations shouldn't be treated as some intellectual exercise that leaves you intellectually restless. The aim should be to satisfy our curiosity about God in order to offer Him our unfettered love."

"I understand and agree. That should be the goal. Can't help it though when my mind wanders off into debilitating questions."

"Such as what?"

"Such as why does it all have to be so difficult? Why do we have to go through these struggles in order to find Him and verify His existence? Why can't He just send us a sign to make it all easy and accessible?" he asked with great frustration.

"Because it is only through difficulty that we get to appreciate anything in this life. We can't enjoy a warm meal unless we're hungry. We can't feel the value of leisure except after exhaustion. Academic success is only meaningful after burning the midnight oil, over long sleepless nights. Our commitment to God is only strong when we treat the endeavour to find Him as a quest for what is loved and lost. Imagine if the signs of God are so blatantly ubiquitous. Everyone would have no reason to believe since it becomes a matter of knowing and not a matter of faith," I answered passionately.

"And what's wrong with that?"

"What's wrong with it is that faith in the existence of what is yet to be discovered is what drives human ingenuity and progress. If we only accept what we have proven, or what we know, there will be no motivation to go beyond. Imagine how this can completely dull human intellect."

"I guess I can see your point. So we basically have to suffer in order to stay sharp?"

"That's one way of putting it!" I said laughingly.

He responded with a long sigh.

"Walk with me. I was told there's a beautiful trail close by," I said as I got up. He followed me as I walked out of the backyard towards a trail next to the house. The trail was beautiful and calming.

A narrow creek meandered on one side, and a treeline blocking any views of man-made structures on the other side. It's as if we were immediately transferred to the wilderness.

"Let's get back to our philosophical debates!" I said with a smile, trying to ease his tension. His mood immediately changed.

"That sounds better! What do you have for me today?"

"The Ontological Argument of Anselm."

He stopped, looked at me with bewilderment, and asked: "the what argument of who?!"

"The Ontological Argument of Anselm," I responded calmly.

"What is ontological? And who's Anselm?"

"Let's cover it one at a time!" I said with a chuckle.

"Okay. Sure. Let's start with the meaning of ontological."

"Ontology is a philosophical branch of metaphysics that studies 'being' through reason. It involves questions such as: what is a being? How does a being come to existence? How does it exist? What is its reality? How can that reality be reached? etc."

"What being are we talking about?"

"In our case: God."

"So what are we trying to study?"

"The ontological arguments try to prove that God exists without relying on any observation of the natural world. As opposed to previous arguments that paid attention to the universe, its beginnings, its components and objects, its causes etc., ontological arguments use solely reason, to establish the being that is God, His existence etc."

"Sounds really complicated…"

"It is. The ontological arguments are the most complicated of all, but they're really effective when you understand them fully."

"Okay…So who's Anselm?"

"Saint Anselm of Canterbury was an Italian monk and philosopher of the 12th century, who formulated one of the first ontological arguments for God."

"So, what does St. Anselm say?"

"This is not going to be easy. Are you ready?" I asked with a smirk.

"What do you mean not easy? Like it's something that will make me queasy, or is it just difficult to process?" he asked cautiously.

"No, the latter!" I said with a loud laugh. "Nothing will turn your stomach here I promise."

"Okay good," he said with a nervous chuckle. "Give it to me!"

"Okay. Here it goes. Anselm says that the idea of God must be better and greater than anything we can ever perceive. Can we agree on this?"

"I guess so, for me at least since I believe in God. What about non-believers?"

"Even non-believers would agree that God, if He were true, He would be the absolute greatest thing ever; greater than whom nothing can be perceived, right?"

"I think so."

"Great. Now Anselm also argues that things exist in either one of two ways: in perception/imagination alone, or in both perception and reality. Does that make sense?"

"I think so. So some things exist only in the mind and not the real world, and other things exist in both, right?"

"Yes! For example, a unicorn belongs to which group?" I asked.

"The things that exist only in the mind I guess. But it's not real, right?" he answered hesitantly.

"It isn't, but that doesn't matter. It's an idea, right? It exists in my mind and yours. Otherwise, we wouldn't be talking about it now!"

"Yes. I understand that."

"Great. So unicorns exist only in perception, right?"

"Right."

"Okay. Now give me an example of something that exists in both perception and reality."

"Well, most things!"

"Granted. Give me one example."

"Okay. Speaking of unicorns, how about a horse?"

"Yes! That's a great example. A horse exists in both perception and reality, as opposed to a unicorn, which only exists in perception, right?"

"Yes!"

"Great. Now Anselm says that the concept of God is an idea that can either exist only in perception, or in both perception and reality. Agreed?"

"Well.. isn't this the whole point? That those who believe in God accept that He exists in reality, and those who don't believe in Him, don't accept that He does?" He asked.

"That's not the point. Whether God exists in reality or not is not relevant here yet. What Anselm is asking us to do is to treat the 'idea' of God like we'd treat any other idea. For some, He is a unicorn, and for others, He's a horse, but either way, the idea of God has to exist in the perception, right?"

"Even for atheists?"

"Of course. Because even if you don't believe in God, or the unicorn, the idea can still exist in the mind, even if it doesn't exist in the real world!"

"Okay. I see it now. Yes! God can either exist in perception, like the unicorn or in both perception and reality, like the horse."

"Fantastic. So to recap: God as an idea is something which no greater can be conceived, using Anselm's language. He also says that ideas can either exist in perception only or in both perception and reality. And since God can at least be an idea, He must exist at least in perception. Good?"

"Yes. Crystal clear!"

"Great. Now, Anselm asks us a very important question. Which is better: an idea that only exists in perception or an idea that exists in both perception and reality?" I asked.

"Umm…. in both perception and reality, I guess?" he answered.

"Why?"

"Because if it exists only in perception, it is incomplete and less useful, while if an idea exists in both perception and reality, it would be complete and most useful! Am I completely off the mark here?" he asked with a weary voice.

"To the contrary! That was a great way to put it! Take the unicorn, for instance. The idea of a unicorn only in perception is as exciting as our imagination can be. It's a cool concept that kids can have dreams about, and perhaps have limited adventures within their minds, but if the unicorn were a reality, it would actually take us to places, and the adventures would be incredible and unbound. Imagine a flying horse actually exists! Which would be better? That unicorns exist only in perception or in both perception and reality?"

"That they exist in both perception and reality of course!"

"You're getting the hang of this!"

"Trust me - my mind is aching. Not used to using that part of my brain."

"Philosophy is incredible."

"I'm just realizing this."

"Okay, back to Anselm. So again, to recap what we discussed lest we forget. Can you share with me in your language what we agreed upon so far?"

"Okay. I'll try. First, God is the greatest thing that can ever be conceived. Second, things can either exist in conception, or in both conception and reality. Third, the idea of God can either exist in conception alone, or in both conception and reality. Fourth, things that exist in both conception and reality are better than things that exist in conception alone - close?"

"Right on the mark!"

"Man!" he said with a sigh of relief.

"Now, Anselm takes us back to God. He says the only thing that could possibly be greater than the existence of God in perception alone is —" he interrupted me before I could finish.

"His existence in both conception and reality!"

"Yes. And this is according to which of Anselm's premises we discussed?"

"The fourth! That things that exist in reality must be better than things that exist in conception only."

"Fabulous! But then Anselm argued that if God exists in perception alone, it would be tantamount to saying that it is possible for something to exist in reality that is greater than that which no greater can ever be perceived, which is absurd."

He stared at me with the most confused face.

"Are you still following?" I asked with a muffled giggle.

He swallowed loudly and said: "barely."

"Where did I lose you? You were doing so well."

"I know, I know. I just couldn't process the last part. Why does Anselm say again that the idea of God in conception alone is absurd?"

"Because according to Anselm, the idea of God is one where no greater idea can be conceived. And if God exists only in conception, then we're basically saying that something else exists in reality that is greater than the idea of God. But this would be like saying: something is greater than the one thing that we just said is the greatest. And this doesn't make sense, right?"

"I think so, but I can't put my thumb fully on it yet."

"Think of it this way. If God, which is the greatest thing that can ever be conceived, exists only in conception, then there is another thing that exists in reality that is greater than the idea of God, right?"

"Yes. I understand this at least."

"But this would be absurd because nothing can be greater than a being that is greater than anything that could ever be conceived, right?"

"Right! If God exists only in conception, when He's supposed to be the greatest thing the mind can ever perceive, then, in reality, there is another entity that is greater than God, which would contradict our first premise, that God is the greatest thing that can ever be conceived."

"Perfect. And if God cannot just exist in conception alone, then what is our conclusion?"

"Then God must exist in reality!"

"There you go!"

"This is the greatest moment of my life!"

I laughed out loud.

"I'm serious. This reasoning was mind-bending but an absolutely exhilarating exercise!"

"Glad you liked it."

"How did other philosophers react to the Ontological Argument?"

"The argument was weaved in different formulations over the centuries. René Descartes, Gottfried Leibniz, and Kurt Gödel have made similar arguments for God, based in Ontology," I said.

"How could anyone possibly refute this reasoning?"

"But they do."

"How?"

"Immanuel Kant, although a believer himself, most famously critiqued the Ontological Argument of Anselm. Kant argues that what makes the argument invalid is its assumption that existence is a predicate."

"What's a predicate?" he asked.

"An essential quality of an entity. So if I said Joe is bald, then being bald is a predicate of Joe. Existence, according to Kant, can't be a predicate - otherwise, if I said God doesn't exist, it would be assumed that God is there, but He lacks the quality of existence."

"Hmm…but this sounds like a play on words. If there is another word to use instead of exist, to allude to the presence of God in the universe, it would make Anselm's argument still valid, right?"

"Agreed. Kant's objection is more technical than substantial. But he's not the only one. Others contend that the Ontological Argument can be used to prove the existence of pretty much everything. Replace the word God with Unicorn, and the argument can still work."

"So, how do we respond to this?"

"Very simple. That Anselm never said that his argument applies to everything. Only an entity that is most perfect, and no greater can ever be perceived. There are many things that can be conceived to be greater than a unicorn, but there's no idea we can ever imagine that would be greater than God."

"This is so nutritional to the brain!"

"Couldn't agree more!"

"Tell me more!"

"Can't. We're already here."

The trail apparently looped around the neighbourhood and brought us back to the house.

"We need to get back to the folks in there before they miss our presence."

"Next time then?"

"Next time, inshaAllah."

## Chapter 5

# Morality

"Imam, I have something amazing to share!" he said frantically on the phone after a brief greeting.

"Happy to hear! Please go right ahead."

"My nephew made contact – again!"

"Very good! Did he call or visit?"

"He texted me the other day and said that he wanted to meet!"

"Did you ask him what it's about?"

"Yes. He said that he has a few questions that are keeping him up at night!"

"This is a good sign. I told you sometimes people need time."

"I know! I'm so happy he's on his way back to the faith."

"Slow down there, chief. I strongly recommend against building high expectations. Your nephew having questions and your nephew returning to the faith are two different things," I said alarmingly.

"I know, I know - I'm just so excited about the prospect of him coming back. His mum is not in very good shape. I keep comforting her but she feels like a total failure."

"We have to keep praying for her and we need to stay the course. The intellectual vacuum that pushed your nephew to the edge of enchantment is not likely to be filled with something solid anytime soon, so we have to keep building those ideas together so that at least you and the family are able to answer his questions and protect other family members and kids from stepping into that territory."

"Agreed. You know I wonder sometimes about how atheism affects not only someone's mind but also their behaviour, ethics, manners etc."

"How so?"

"Think about it. When my nephew lost his faith, not only did he develop an intellectual problem with God or religion, his very behaviour changed."

"In what sense?" I asked inquisitively.

"He just overall became rude, dismissive, and even arrogant. This is so not how he was. It breaks my heart to see how he doesn't even check on his mum."

"Well, he just made contact recently, so that's a good thing, right?"

"I guess. He reached out to me because he still has questions, but he doesn't ask about his mum."

"Perhaps he's embarrassed," I suggested.

"Perhaps, but I think losing faith is synonymous with losing your moral compass. You simply cannot remain a moral person once you've lost your faith. Moral behaviour is derived from God. You lose God, you lose your manners!"

"There might be some philosophical truth to what you're saying but I think it's a lot less severe than you think."

"It is not possible to live a moral life if you don't believe in God, is it?"

"Well, I actually think it is possible. Many atheists can live a moral life and be good people," I said cautiously.

"So you're saying that morality can still exist if God doesn't? That wouldn't make sense. What would the source of that morality be?"

"Listen. If the question is: can people be moral without believing that God exists, the answer is yes. Atheists can define a moral code and successfully adhere to its boundaries. They do that all the time. Living a moral life brings a host of benefits to individuals and society, regardless of one's acceptance of God. But if the question is: can people be moral in a universe where God doesn't exist, the answer would be an emphatic: no!"

"Interesting. So what you're saying is that morality comes from

God and even if people choose not to believe in God they can still follow that morality and enjoy its benefits. But if God doesn't exist, there would be no morality to follow, right?"

"Yes, with a minor modification. I would add the word objective before morality."

"Objective morality? What is the difference?" he asked.

"Everyone can subjectively create a regimen of habits and call it morality. Objective morality is universally applicable, and is not bound by spatial and temporal limitations."

"Spatial and temporal? Can you please use less complicated words for the uncultured like me?"

"Of course!" I said with a chuckle. "Temporal is related to time and spatial is related to space. What I meant to say is that objective morality is universally valid and applicable, and most decent human beings agree with its validity and binding nature across time and space. In every generation and in any country, most people would agree that murder, lying, and sleeping with your friend's wife, or taking the wealth of orphans are terrible acts. You don't need dogma to teach you that. Atheists and theists alike would both agree that such objective morality is real and it exists everywhere."

"Fascinating. I definitely see the difference."

"Its actually very interesting that Muslim theologians debated matters of morality and God over 1200 years ago." I said.

"This is very interesting. Tell me more?"

"Well, the question that theologians raised was this: if an act is good, is it so because it carries an innate quality that makes it good, or is it good because it was designated as such by God?"

"Not following," he said.

"Let's take lying for instance. It is considered to be an immoral act for most of us. Is it immoral because it carries an innate quality of immorality embedded within, or is it immoral because God said so?"

"Hmm…hard to answer this question. You would assume that God will only call something bad because it is. But on the other hand, God can do whatever He wants, and can accordingly make something immoral if He wants to."

"This was precisely the nature of the moral debate between the Ash'ari and the Mu'tazali schools. The latter held that God chose a certain action because it was inherently moral, and the former held that actions become moral when chosen by God. The Mu'tazalis seem to have believed in the existence of objective morality independent of God, whereas the Ash'aris believed that acts are only moral when God makes them so, otherwise, if He so willed, He would have designated them differently."

"Wait, does this mean that in a sense God could have created another universe in which lying is moral?" he asked with great curiosity.

"The Ash'aris would certainly say so," I answered.

"But wait - doesn't this make morality kind of arbitrary? Like things are a certain way only because God said so, and not because of a quality of their own?"

"The Mu'tazalis would probably agree with you on this arbitrariness question, but not the Ash'aris. The problem with an objective morality independent of God is that it almost commits God to something He created. So He brings to existence people and grants them a moral sense and moral systems to follow, and imbues morality in certain actions, and now becomes committed to uphold those actions," I said.

"I can see how this can be troubling. It would make less sense if we assume that God creates a boundary and then becomes limited by that boundary. And if God allows for immoral acts to be carried out, then God permits something immoral to happen and violates His boundaries, and that can adversely affect people's faith," he said astutely.

"Precisely! This is perhaps why it would make more sense to accept an objective moral sense, but still assuming that it was made so by God, as opposed to a morality that is independent of the Creator's classification."

"Let me ask you though: how can morality be used to make a

case for God?" he asked.

"Actually, all arguments that use objective morality to make a case for God's existence are called the Moral Arguments for God" I answered.

"Sounds simple enough. I'm thirsty for more."

"The moral argument was first propounded through the great Christian philosopher and theologian Thomas Aquinas. His argument was simple: we 'grade' moral behaviour all the time. When faced with two actions that are good, we comfortably decide that one is 'more moral' than the other. For instance, if you have to choose between saving a calf and a child from drowning, saving a child would be of a higher moral order, right?"

"I would think so, yes," he answered.

"And if we can 'grade' things in this way, then we are -at least implicitly- comparing them to some absolute standard from which the very definitions of right and wrong, and their grading are derived. Aquinas argues that this standard is only possible if there is some Being which possesses these qualities in their most perfect form."

"And obviously that being would be God?"

"That's what Aquinas clearly argues. God would have to be not only the most perfect manifestation of these qualities but also the cause of them."

"This is powerful," he said pensively.

"I know for you as a man of faith it makes sense, but Aquinas' arguments rest upon a lot of assumptions that needed to be proven in and of themselves, at least as far as philosophers are concerned."

"So how did that play out?"

"Theistic philosophers tackled this argument over the centuries. Its best formulations were probably iterated by Immanuel Kant. Kant contended that any decent human being who possesses rationality and a moral character must necessarily desire "the highest good," which consists of a world in which people are both morally good and happy. In this world, the path to happiness would be moral virtue."

"Sorry to interrupt, but I want to make sure I understand. So Kant says that human beings by nature desire to achieve this moral excellence, which is to be in a world where people live happily *because* they make moral choices, right?"

"A great way to summarise it!"

"Great. Please continue."

"So Kant held that a person cannot rationally desire this happy life without believing that moral actions can successfully achieve such an end, and this requires a belief that the universe is designed to achieve this end by moral means. This is equivalent to belief in God, a moral Being who is ultimately responsible for the universe and the natural world."

"So, if I desire a happy life that is an end product of moral behaviour, I need to believe that God exists in order to reward that moral behaviour with happiness? Isn't that like wishful thinking?"

"How?" I asked.

"He's basically saying that God *needs* to exist in order to grant a reward for moral choices. But the need for God's existence doesn't prove that existence, does it?"

"That's not what Kant is saying. His argument is that most people agree that objective morality exists and that if most of us followed it, it would lead to happiness for most. Most of us do follow that paradigm in our dealings and interactions. For Kant, this is an indication that deep inside, all of us are programmed to accept that there must be a universal standard for this moral behaviour that makes it objective and that the source of that standard will ultimately reward moral behaviour. Whether we admit it or not, that standard has to be God."

"I get it. Of course, this sounds plausible to me, but I can see how this can be rendered weak by some atheists."

"I do too, and that's why many philosophers attempted to buttress Kant's moral arguments, by invoking the 'moral command' argument."

"What is that?"

"Henry Newman argues that we follow man-made laws all the time. They tell us what to do and what not to do. Those man-made laws act like 'commands' that we follow. The source of those commands being the body that enacted the laws, such as legislative entities or absolute monarchs etc. They become the 'commander' so to speak. When one feels remorse after committing an immoral act or feels fulfilled after performing something that is morally superior, those feelings reflect that there is a 'commander' of moral acts that I unconsciously worry about His possible reward and punishment. It's a sense of accountability that we possess towards the ultimate commander of morality. Most humans, across culture and geography, possess those innate feelings."

"So the assumption is that the Commander is God right?"

"Yes."

"Interesting. It does make sense, although I still see how the premises of the arguments and the conclusion may not be entirely airtight."

"You're developing a good philosophical sense! Glad you're getting the hang of this!"

"Thanks to you!"

"You're absolutely right. The premises do not yield a definitive conclusion. Only that God is a bigger probability than not-God. The moral argument has force that cannot be ignored, but establishing the probability of God's existence is not as strong as establishing God's existence," I concluded.

"Interesting. It is obvious to me nonetheless, that there's a code of morals ingrained in all of us, across cultures, religions, and races. This has been the case for millennia, before the internet and social media. This code of morality is so commonplace and conspicuous that it can't just be dismissed. I think that's clear enough to me," he said.

"True. But I have something else to add to this. It may just add a little more force, but certainly doesn't provide any definitive conclusions."

"What is it?"

"Atheists argue that morality can be explained through secular means as a necessary condition for social solidarity and group survival. Regardless of how we explain morality, I believe that people who are moral are generally at a disadvantage, compared to those who are not."

"Hmm…why do you think so?" he asked.

"Think about it. Morality teaches self-sacrifice, altruism, and putting other people's interests before ours. You strive for some greater good. You aspire for otherworldly gains etc. These considerations compel moral people to let things go, forgive, focus on sublime gains, the greater good, and so forth. What should that do to them in the long term?"

"Not sure…trouble?"

"A lot of trouble. My point is that moral behaviour should generally make moral people weaker, simply because they're not willing to go the extra distance that immoral people are willing to go."

"I can definitely see what you mean. Immoral people will kill, steal and maim to have what they want, and they might eventually become superior to moral people, who are not willing to use immoral methods to achieve their ends."

"Precisely, and what does the theory of natural selection say about weaker members of a group?" I asked.

"That they will gradually wither away right. Survival of the fittest!"

"Exactly! In a material world, where God doesn't exist, moral people should gradually disappear because they will be outwitted and out-maneuvered by immoral people who are willing to take all measures necessary to achieve their goals. But this clearly is not the case in our world. Moral people still thrive everywhere. In fact, most people follow some morality one way or the other."

"But what if someone says that strict laws prevent immoral people from hurting others or infringing upon their rights, and that's why moral people still survive?"

"I would say that human ingenuity knows no bounds. Despite very strict laws, immoral people will still find ways and loopholes to have what is not theirs. Over extended periods of time, millennia as natural selection would have it, the immoral still holds an advantage over the moral, and therefore the moral will get weaker and get weeded out, which is clearly not the case in our world. But this is not just about protecting a silent, passive moral minority. Moral people are active in their efforts to make the world better, sometimes at their own expense. Members of society cooperate and collaborate. They make sacrifices and issue each other charitable forgiveness. They often deny self-benefit to the advantage of social progress. They fight wars for the love of country and die in the line of duty to protect and serve. Our collective social experience is not indicative of the self-centred, ruthlessly violent, and unforgiving process of natural selection. There has to be more at play here than strict laws."

"And what is the conclusion then to this premise?"

"That God is proven, not only through the mere presence of objective morality but also through the actions of moral people who still thrive in a world in which they should have disappeared a long time ago if evolutionary selection was the only way to explain things."

"This is astounding!"

"Glad you enjoyed our discussion."

"Do you think I should bring up the morality question to my nephew when we meet?"

"I wouldn't. Only if he brings it up."

"Great advice! Thank you."

"You're welcome."

"Pray for him, and for me!"

"I will. See you next time!"

*Chapter 6*

# Evolution

"Imam, Assalamu'alaikum. There's a brother here to see you," our office manager said as she peeked into my office.

"I don't recall scheduling any meetings right now," I said.

"Yes, he says there's no appointment, but he says it's urgent."

"Let him in please." I had to put aside my *khutba* preparation, and wait for this unanticipated guest. He finally showed up at the door, barged into the room. It was the uncle.

"Imam…I have bad news," he blurted out.

"Oh boy…what happened? Are you okay?"

"I had a meeting with my nephew," he said with anxiety.

"Please have a seat and catch your breath." He sat down restlessly.

"Tell me about the meeting with your nephew. How did it go?" I asked.

"Not that good," he answered while shaking his head.

"How come? Tell me. It's okay. Nothing we cannot fix."

"I don't want to sound like a complainer, but I don't think there's any hope left."

"But that is not for us to decide now is it?"

"I know, but I can see the signs. You know the *hikmah* keychain you gave him? He possesses none of that!" he said angrily.

"Please try to calm down. What signs do you see?"

"He's being stubborn and all he does is keep finding flaws in religious foundations and arguments."

"But isn't that what he's supposed to do when he's struggling with this faith? What do you expect him to do?"

"I expect a little respect at least!" he said loudly.

"Arguing about religion is not disrespectful. Remember, we failed this generation before they failed us. If you see the style of writing of the likes of Richard Dawkins and Sam Harris, versus some of the things religious thinkers write and articulate nowadays, you'll understand the gravity of the situation," I said.

"I know, I know - I guess I just feel that I'm so not prepared for this stuff," he said with great frustration.

"Neither of us are, but we have to try. Perhaps the rise of atheism is the impetus that we need in order to jolt life back into religious thought. Let's think of this as an opportunity."

"What becomes of my nephew though? What if he dies in this state? Will he be removed from God's mercy?"

"Let's not think in these apocalyptic terms. Only God adjudicates these matters. There's no need to burden yourself with more depressing thoughts. Just focus on the mission here," I said while looking him straight in the eyes.

"But what is the mission?" he asked.

"To use this dialogue to generate sound ideas that may help your nephew find his way back to the faith, and prevent others from losing it."

"I agree. The points he raised in our conversation really offended me though!"

"Why did they?"

"Because his statements were a straight assault on all my beliefs and everything I took for granted since I was a child."

"Give me one example."

"Well, he says religious scriptures make it very clear: Adam and Eve are the first humans, and they existed around 8,000 years ago when they came down to earth from heaven. In reality, he says, humans have roamed the earth for close to 200,000 years! There's no such thing as Adam and Eve he says! It's all religious fabrication he says! It made me so mad…"

"But he kind of has a point doesn't he?" I said cautiously.

"A point? As in Adam and Eve never existed and we are all descendants of apes?! How can we accept such nonsense?" he asked with a resentful tone.

"I'm not saying you have to accept it. Just find a rational way to refute it, or reconcile it with religious truths."

"How can this evolution nonsense ever be reconciled with religion? Evolution and creation are mutually exclusive, aren't they?"

"Not necessarily," I said calmly.

"I'm going crazy over here Imam! How can a paradigm where God created man, and another paradigm where man is a descendant of monkeys, be one and the same?"

I laughed.

"It's not funny I swear!" he said with controlled rage.

"I don't mean to make light of this point. I'll address it later I promise. What else did he say?"

"He kept hammering me with the theory of evolution and how it's sufficient to explain the origin of life, and how God is effectively dead!"

"I can see how that would be seriously hurtful."

"It is, and I don't know if I can handle another meeting with him to be quite honest."

"Trust me you will, and it'll be a lot easier than this one. Let's just unpack what he said piece by piece and see how to address it."

"That's why I'm here," he said with a sigh.

"So in your nephew's mind, the idea of God has been revoked by which world view?"

"Evolution, right?"

"No. The competing worldview to creation is not evolution. It's naturalism."

"And what is naturalism?"

"It's the philosophical view that only through the observation of nature and the hypotheses of science that all forms of truth can be ascertained. There's nothing beyond human perception. And in this view, evolution and Darwinism are views of science that are entirely sufficient to explain the world. There is nothing that resides beyond what we can, and will potentially perceive through the senses."

"Can evolution be seen in a different light?"

"Indeed. It can be seen as a theory of science that has useful applications, one that explains the biodiversity of the world and speaks to the interconnectedness of all species. But to take evolution and turn it into a philosophical worldview, would take a lot more than science to achieve."

"You seem to be using evolution and Darwinism interchangeably. Are they the same?" he asked.

"Not entirely. Evolution is a perspective of science that describes the biological process by which species change overtime. As members of a certain species reproduce, cumulative, gradual changes happen overtime, that lead to changes within the species, and the formation of new species, also known as speciation. Darwinism, on the other hand, is a comprehensive theory of science propounded by Charles Darwin that uses evolution to explain the origin and diversity of life."

"So what's involved in Darwinism beyond evolution?"

"Well, Darwinism not only describes the process of change through evolution, it argues that that change happens over an extremely long time, measured in thousands, if not millions of years, called deep time. It also describes the mechanics of evolutionary change. Darwin perpetuated the notion of natural selection, in which the environment favours the species that adapts, while others die out. In addition to that, Darwinism argues that evolution, by consequence, proves the common ancestry of all species. We can all fit into a long family tree of life that leads to one common ancestor, which is likely a mono-cellular organism.

"So Darwinism involves evolution, deep time, natural selection and common ancestry?"

"Accurately put," I answered with a smile.

"But I studied in college other perspectives, such as genetic mutations and fossil records etc."

"Well, at the time of Darwin, the science of genetics was not yet in existence and the fossil record was limited and choppy. In the later decades of the 20ᵗʰ century, scientists started finding further evidence for evolution in both genetics and the fossil record. They also used homology, which is the science of shared features between species, to further prove that evolution was valid. These modern perspectives are called Neo-Darwinism."

"Interesting."

"Last but not least, is the distinction between micro and macro evolution."

"Which is?" he asked.

"Microevolution describes the changes that happen within a certain species overtime to further that species' adaptability to the environment. This includes changes in the colour of the skin, the function of certain organs, or adjustments that happen to the size overtime to make an animal most suited and fitted to its environment. Macroevolution describes the process of evolving from one species to the other."

"How is that possible?"

"Well, a species generally represents members of a certain class of animals that can mate together. Due to cataclysmic events, members of the same species get separated, and start undergoing different processes of microevolution within their divided groups. Over millions of years, that microevolution will change the genotype and phenotype of the species so much so that they cannot mate with the other group anymore. This is called macroevolution, and it leads to the creation of a new species, or speciation."

"I appreciate the summary you just gave me about evolution and Darwinism. This still cannot be acceptable Islamically right?"

"Why not?"

"Because a perspective that suggests we all evolved from primitive ancestors cannot be reconciled with our views about how God created the universe and everything in it, including every individual species! After all, it's just a theory, and the fossil record is choppy at best," he said with muffled anger.

"This is way too general a statement. We have to qualify our contentions in order not to sound anti-scientific and naive."

"And how do we achieve this?"

"First, we have to ask ourselves this question: what is it exactly that our religious sensibilities struggle with when it comes to evolution? Darwinism, whether classical or neo, involves many processes. Let's discuss them one by one and see which ones we're actually having a problem with."

"Fair enough."

"Great. First, do we have a problem with deep time?" I asked.

"I suppose not. Although the scriptures suggest that Adam walked the earth about 8,000 years ago."

"This is actually not true. It may be a Biblical perspective, but it certainly is not a Quranic paradigm. There is no mention in the Quran about a time frame for Adam whatsoever. And if this is the case, is the Quran compatible with the possibility that man may have walked the earth for tens of thousands of years?"

"I guess so."

"Great. Moreover, are we okay with the age of the earth?" I asked.

"You mean that it's millions of years old?"

"Yes."

"I don't see a problem with that."

"And since there is nothing in the Quran that indicates the actual age of the earth, is it safe to say that we as Muslims are fine with deep time?"

"I suppose we are." He answered.

"Great. Let me jump into the second premise of Darwinism. Are we okay with micro-evolution?"

"I guess changes that happen within a species over time are way too obvious to ignore."

"Great. I agree. So we're okay with deep time and micro-evolution, right?"

"Yes we are."

"Let me then ask you. Are we okay with macro evolution?"

"You mean species coming into existence?"

"Precisely," I answered.

"Well, I'm not sure about this one. It's God that creates things right? How can the idea that species came into existence through random mutations and natural selection be compatible with our understanding of God's wisdom and His divine plan?"

"I will respond to your point about randomness later, but let me address the notion of compatibility first. Is there anything in the scripture that describes the methodology of creation?"

"What do you mean methodology?" he asked confusedly.

"I mean does the Quran actually describe in detail 'how' God creates things?"

"Well, not sure."

"The Quran usually describes at length the fact that God created the diversity of life on earth, but it doesn't say how. It only alludes to the origins of everything, which is the Arabic word تراب *Turab*, or the dirt of the earth. It certainly doesn't describe how it all happens. Is it possible that slow, methodic evolution over time could be one of many possible processes by which God brings life into existence?"

"I guess so. But it's still thin. God talks about the 'be and it is' paradigm frequently in the Quran."

"But 'be and it is' doesn't necessarily suggest the instant sprouting of a being into existence. God in the Quran talks about how man is the product of 'be and it is' yet it takes us, and all creation really, actual time - in our case nine months - to come into existence. And if that is the case, then the evolution of one species from another could be one possible way by which God 'creates'. And if so, can we at least say that the Quran is not inherently or clearly opposed to macro evolution?" I asked curiously.

"I guess not, based on what you just described. Still controversial though," he said while shaking his head with hesitation.

"I understand. But considering the overwhelming support for Darwinisim in the scientific community, and how much pinning it against religious belief caused many faithful to renounce their faith, it might be wise to avoid fighting every battle and focus on what seems to be a deal breaker."

"This is not unwise," he conceded.

"Great. Now let's move on to a more controversial tenet of evolution. Are we okay with common ancestry?"

"Meaning that we and the apes have the same ancestor?"

"Well, meaning that all living things on earth are somehow connected and that we all hailed from one single living organism," I said with a chuckle.

"Absolutely not. There is no religious person that would agree with us sharing an ancestor with apes, donkeys and frogs," he said with determination.

"Let me make this a little easier. Are we okay with all life on earth, except humans, sharing a common ancestor? Does it bother our religious sensibilities that horses and zebras are related? Or that hippos and whales may have a common ancestor?"

"I guess the Quran is not explicit in its denial of that commonality. It certainly would be opposed to Adam being a part of this process though," he said firmly.

"Great. So what you're saying is that we are okay with almost all Darwinian premises: deep time, micro and macroevolution, natural selection, genetic mutations, and even common ancestry, with the exclusion of man, right?"

"Well, when you put it this way I guess I'm going to have to agree. It seems that Darwinism is religiously admissible, with the exception of its perspective on the origin of man."

"Great. By the way, let me make something clear here before we proceed," I stated with caution.

"What is it?" he asked curiously.

"I'm not saying that evolution or Darwinism is valid. This is for scientists to decide. It's possible that hundreds of years from today with more scientific discoveries that we will find a more accurate perspective to explain biodiversity and the origin of life. All I'm saying is that Darwinism as it stands today, with the exception of Adam being a part of the common ancestry of biological life, is not incompatible with Islamic religious teachings. That's what we agreed upon, right?"

"Yes. I see the distinction and I agree with your statement. Still though, I'm having a hard time accepting how a process that depends entirely on chance can be reconciled with the intentionality of God's creation!"

"Aha. Let me talk about chance and probability," I said with excitement.

"By all means," he said skeptically.

"Let me ask you this. What is a random chance in your judgement?"

"That an event takes place arbitrarily and that it was equally possible for that event to happen any other way."

"Not a bad definition. What's a good example of an event in your judgment?" I asked.

"Well, a coin toss for instance," he answered.

"This is a great example. Let's talk about a coin toss. This is usually used as the typical example of random chance right? It's always either heads or tails," I asked.

"Yes it is," he answered.

"Well, wouldn't you agree that whether a coin toss is heads or tails, is dependent on wind speed, strength of the toss, friction of the ground etc. and a host of other factors that we simply cannot account for?"

"Correct," he said cautiously.

"Great. Is it impossible for us to one day develop a computer algorithm that can accurately take into consideration every possible available factor that can determine the outcome of a coin toss and predict with precision which side the coin will fall on?"

"Yes, I think so!" he said.

"In other words, is it safe to say that the outcome of a coin toss is not really arbitrary at all, and that the reason we call it chance is because we don't understand all the factors that determine the outcome?"

"I think I agree with this. Where are we going with it though?"

"That the evolutionary process, although it involves what we might consider random processes of natural selection and random genetic mutations, is not actually random at all, and that they are subject to a plethora of factors, of which we simply have no knowledge, and that's why we, out of mental laziness, call it random chance."

"It's possible, yes."

"Can we then say that the mechanics of evolution, although they may seem random to us because of our lack of knowledge, may simply be a process that is guided by the hands of a creator?"

"I see what you're saying! I guess I'm going to have to agree with this!" he said with excitement.

"Great. So we're okay with every Darwinian premise so far except the origin of Adam, right?"

"Not so fast. We didn't talk about the moral consequences of Darwinism. Why would a loving God create all kinds of species and a diverse biological world and then destroy it through disasters and violent extinctions? Why is there so much evil in the world? Doesn't it say in the scripture that the world was in peace and it was Adam's sin that started evil basically?"

"I'll address the porblem of evil later, but for now, let me just say that you're confusing Christian and Muslim theology again," I said.

"How come?"

"There is no mention in the Quran that the world lived in peace before man. In fact, in God's conversation with the angels as he announced to them the creation of Adam, they pointed out the fact that there was carnage and bloodshedd on earth.[2] Besides, the

Quran talks about no original sin. We all come to this world pure and our actions determine our destiny."

"Be that as it may, it still doesn't explain why God subjects millions of species to violent extinctions."

"Well, we have to decide on something: are we willing to subject God to our moral sensibilities as the human race, and pretend to have full knowledge of the wisdom behind divine action, or not?" I asked.

"Well, the answer would be no I suppose. God created morality and is not limited by its scope, just like time, space etc. Also we can't really know about all the things that God does, and why He does them."

"Precisely. It would not be prudent to somehow use the pretenses of human morality that changes through time and is influenced by culture and other factors, and try to contain God, or make assumptions about His action within that human moral framework. The Ash'ari school of thought in the Islamic tradition is clear on this. An action is good not because it has an inherent quality that makes it good. Rather, a good action is such because God classified it as such. This way, we liberate ourselves from making assumptions about God and His actions. If it was necessary in His wisdom to bring extinction upon millions of species, then be it. We don't know God's intentions and may not alway understand His wisdom. Causing a species to suffer is considered bad in human moral language, but the same may not apply to God's actions, since He is not subject to the limitations of our moral systems. I will discuss the problem of evil in general at length later though."

"You always have a way to wiggle out of a dilemma!" he said with a nervous chuckle.

"It is not wiggling out! I'm just trying to confine the battle with evolution to the minimum, otherwise we'll be fighting on multiple fronts and we're doomed to fail."

"I see where you're coming from," he conceded.

"So let's recap. We find Darwinism compatible with faith as far as most of its premises are concerned: deep time, micro and macroevolution, natural selection and genetic mutations, randomness and chance, and its moral implications."

"Yes we do, I think."

"The only sticky issue with Darwinism seems to be the story of Adam, right?"

"Yes. The Quran is clear. Adam was created by God in heaven, and brought down to earth. There is no way this can be reconciled with Darwinian common ancestry. There is not a man of faith who would concede to the claim that Adam is a descendant of apes."

"Let's dissect these statements together. But before that, I need to make distinctions between Christian and Islamic perspectives on creation."

"I'm all ears," he said.

"First, the Bible assigns actual dates and time frames to the story of life. The earth was created about 10,000 years ago, and Adam was created around 6000 years BC. There was peace on earth, and everything was beautiful and sinless. God then decided to create Adam, in the Garden of Eden. God's plan was for Adam and his descendants to stay in heaven, so He created for him his mate Eve, from one of his ribs. He lived with Eve in the Garden until Satan whispered to Eve to eat from the forbidden tree. The tree would have given them eternal life, and so God forbade them from touching it. Curious, the couple eventually ate from the tree. It angered God so much that He punished them by expelling them from the Garden of Eden, from paradise basically, and sent them to earth to suffer. And as Adam sinned, suffering and pain were brought to this earth. Everything else is history."

"This sounds about right," he said.

"Here's the thing though. This Christian view commits Christiantiy as a whole to reject evolution and Darwinism. They're certainly not conceptually compatible. You cannot argue that the earth was created 10,000 years ago, and 3 millions years ago at the same time. You cannot reconcile the relative peace on earth before

Adam with the relative carnage on earth before and after Adam. This is why there's a large number of Christians who consider their faith to be at odds with evolution, and developed opposing schools of thought, such as young earth creationism, old earth creationism, intelligent design etc."

"I can definitely see how the Christian perspective would be incompatible with Darwinism. The problem is that I always thought the Christian and Muslim perspectives are identical in this particular regard!"

"Can't think of anything farther from the truth," I said.

"How come?"

"Well, for starters, the Quran does not commit itself to any dates. There's nothing that suggests an actual age of the earth. Even the idea of creating the universe in 'six days'[3] can be understood as six actual 24-hour earth days, or six units of time that may be significantly longer than six days. In one verse the Quran states that the Day of Judgement is equivalent to 50,000 years of our days[4]. In another, the Quran states that it's equivalent to a thousand of our years.[5] This goes to show that the word 'day' in the Quran means a unit of time, and not particularly the earth day."

"Fascinating!" he exclaimed.

"Moreover, in the Quran, God seems to inform the angels of His plans prior to executing them. He declares to them that it was His intention to create man to become His vicegerent on earth.[6] As if making man God's trustee on this earth was the intended outcome of the story of creation from its very beginning."

"Wait, if God's intention was to keep Adam on earth, does that mean God always wanted to expel him and Eve from *Jannah*?"

"No. It means that Adam and Eve were never in *Jannah* in the first place!" I said firmly.

"Wait, what? I've never heard of this before. I was taught that Adam and Eve were in paradise together and then God expelled them and sent them down to earth in order to punish them, bringing this punishment on the rest of us basically!"

"This is precisely why I'm trying to distinguish between the Muslim and the Christian perspectives. What you described is not compatible with the Quranic narrative. Let's disect it further. First, as I mentioned earlier, it was God's intention for man to be His trustee on earth. This is not in-line with the assumption that man was supposed to be somewhere else."

"Hmm, I can see how this would be incompatible. But what does that mean? Wasn't Adam created in *Jannah*?"

"This leads me to my second point. The word *Jannah* doesn't just mean paradise or the Garden of Eden in which the righteous will dwell in the afterlife. The word simply means a hidden garden in the Arabic language. Paradise is *the* garden. But not every *Jannah* is paradise. *Jannah* could be any hidden dwelling in which God created Adam and Eve and kept them there for a while."

"Wait, where would that ordinary garden be then?"

"On earth."

"What?" he asked in shock.

"The garden, or *Jannah* in which Adam and Eve were created, was on earth. They stayed there for as long as Allah wanted, for them to be ready, and when they became ready, they were sent out to the world to become God's trustees, as was intended from the beginning."

"The strangest thing I've ever heard," he responded while shaking his head in disbelief.

"Is it really that hard to accept? God said He wanted man to be His trustee on earth. He also said that He created all of us from the dirt of the earth, and that it is to the earth we shall all return.[7] Satan was allowed to whisper to Adam and Eve in that garden, when the Quran says that he was already expelled from paradise.[8] He can't be expelled from a place by God, and then allowed to enter again and plot against God's favourite creation."

"It's as if I'm hearing the story of creation for the first time!" he said with astonishment.

"More importantly, understanding the story in this light affords

God the intentionality and the foreknowledge that befit His grace and omniscience. There is no way Satan snuck into paradise to whisper to Adam and Eve without God's knowledge, and there is no way God was surprised by Adam's disobedience. This must all be part of the plan."

"Fascinating, but what does this have to do with evolution then?"

"I will explain that later. Just wanted to set the proper backdrop before we proceed. Making a distinction between Christain theological assumptions and the Quranic narrative is important. Most modern day friction between religion and science is generated by Christian theology and not Islam. This disentanglement is necessary to avoid fighting battles we don't need to fight."

"Great. I appreciate this perspective," he said with content.

"Glad to hear. Let me go back to Darwinism and faith. We agreed that we're okay with most all Neo-Darwinian premises, except the origin of Adam, right?"

"Yes!"

"Great. Let me explore with you the different Islamic schools of thought with regard to this matter. I need to do this for the purposes of showing you that perhaps there is no incompatibility between Darwinsims and at least some Islamic views."

"Let me have it!" he said with excitement.

"First, there are traditional Muslim creationists, much like Christian creationists, who beleive that Adam, and perhaps all other species, were created through the direct will of God into their individual species, and that no evolution took place in the biological world, at lest not in its macro sense."

"Yes, and this is the traditional view."

"But one that is most likely to be at odds with science, and we've discussed earlier how committing to this view might be unjustified and even harmful."

"Agreed. Denying evolution categorically is not useful."

"Great. Then there is a school of thought that is called 'Human Exceptionalism'". In this school, evolution, with all its Darwinian premises is admissible, except when it comes to human beings."

"Interesting. Can you detail their position a bit and why?"

"Sure. While human exceptionalists are willing to accept Darwinism in general, they believe that man was created miraculously by God and was brought down to this earth. All biological life may have been subjected to the impact of the evolutionary machine, except human beings."

"Interesting. And how do they justify the similarities between man and other primates, and the fact that human beings seem to be perfectly placed in the evolutionary ladder?"

"Well, the argument is that right at the historic moment when lower humanoids were supposed to evolve into human beings, God placed the first man right there. They often use the dominoes example to illustrate their point."

"And what is that?" He asked.

"Imagine so many pieces of dominoes placed in sequence, close enough to each other that when the first one topples the rest will follow. Now imagine all the pieces toppled and then someone placed a piece at the very end. If a spectator who did not witness the toppling of the dominoes looked at the pieces, they would have no way to ascertain whether the last piece toppled with the process, or was deliberately placed there."

"Interesting! So let me get this straight. Human Exceptionalists argue that while evolution is a biological fact, humans were not subjected to it, since the first man, Adam, was created by God and placed on earth at that opportune moment when humans were naturally going to arise from the evolutionary process?"

"This pretty much sums it up" I said.

"Wow. So through this thought process we basically stay authentic as far as Islamic theology is concerned, while dodging the bullet of evolution."

"I suppose Human Exceptionalists would agree with you."

"But you don't, right?" he asked curiously.

"Well, my main issue with this perspective is that, while it does manage to protect a perceived notion in Islamic orthodoxy, it somehow manages to dilute both science and theology by offering the unfalsifiable answer to anything: it was a miracle. In the presence of a perfectly justifiable scientific theory, it's hard for most to just dismiss it and cling to an obscure religious explanation. So I suppose all Human Exceptionalism does is that it protects the dogma of the faithful, which is still useful, but it's not positioned to engage any non-faithful in a meaningful dialogue. It's a conversation-ender so to speak."

"I see your point, but it's still brilliant though. Sometimes all we need to protect our kids' minds to show them that there are multiple ways. Human Exceptionalism provides an alternative at least."

"Agreed. It is valuable for sure," I said contently.

"What other perspectives do we have?" he asked with excitement.

"Well, there is what came to be known as Adamic Exceptionalism," I answered.

"Wow! That sounds super brilliant! What is Adamic Exceptionalism?"

"Just like Human Exceptionalism, all Darwinian premises are admissible except when applied to human beings. But the difference is that, while Human Exceptionalism argues that ALL humans are an exception to the evolutionary process —"

He interrupted me with excitement and blurted out: "Adamic Exceptionalisms says it was only Adam, right?"

"Someone is becoming a secret philosopher!" I said with a big smile.

"For real!"

"You're right. Adamic Exceptionalism suggests that while it's possible that there were other humans that came to existence through the evolutionary process, Adam in particular was a miracle from God, and was placed on earth at a certain point."

"Absolutely fascinating! So only Adam was a miracle in this perspective?"

"Yes. That's what they would argue," I answered.

"But wait. What became of the other non-Adamic humans? Are their descendants still around? Doesn't that make some of us not trace our ancestry to Adam?"

"Precisely. And that's why Adamic Exceptionalsits argue that either the non-Adamic bloodlines went extinct, making Adam's descendants the only surviving humans, or that some of the other bloodlines survived, but only the one that Adam's descendants mated with."

"Wait, wouldn't that suggest that some of us are descendants of Adam and some are not? Aren't all of us supposed to be from Adam in Islamic theology?"

"Well, when you think about it, even if some of us are not purely of Adamic ancestry, meaning we didn't come directly from Adam and Eve, if we still have Adamic blood, at least on one side, we're still all, one way or the other, descendants of Adam."

"What an astounding perspective!" he stated with amazement.

"It's an effective perspective to still uphold Darwinism, while being loyal to the fundamental premise that Adam was a miraculous creation of God placed on earth at the right time."

"Knowing you though, I feel that you're not entirely convinced with this perspective."

"Not entirely, no," I said with a smirk.

"Why?"

"Well, I do believe that it's a powerful and innovative narrative, but leaves more to be desired. First, if humans already roamed the earth, what's the point of God sending one that totally resembles them in every way? Why allow for the evolutionary process to take its course, and produce human beings, and then send another one from heavens? To achieve what?"

"To achieve the purpose of making us all descendants of a beautiful miracle of God!"

"That's my point. It seems that Adamic Exceptionalism is mostly about ideological fidelity. It serves no other purpose but to show that we all came from Adam, but the evolutionary process could have just as effectively done that, without God's intervention. It almost feels redundant."

"I see your point;" he said pensively.

"Second, it equates the evolutionary process with God's direct creation in value. Earth had humans that were intelligent and morally conscious, and then God created a human being that was also intelligent and morally conscious. How then is Adam a miracle if he shares the same traits with other humans?"

"Interesting perspective. I suppose there is a perspective that you are more inclined to support?"

"As a matter of fact there is. And it's a perspective that I personally have been developing, although it hasn't been published yet."

"Now my curiosity is going through the roof!"

"This perspective I call 'Adamic Intellectual Endowment'.""

"Sounds super sophisticated! What is it about?" he asked.

"Well, here goes. We agree that it was God's original plan for Adam and Eve to live on earth, right?" I asked.

"Right."

"Good. So the story starts with God telling the angels that He plans to create Adam. How does it end?"

"With Adam and Eve coming down to earth disgraced after they ate from the tree."

"I will accept that. What happened in between?" I asked him.

"Well, God commanded the angels to bow to Adam, and Satan refused. Then God punished Satan by banishing him from heaven. Then Adam and Eve roamed heaven freely, and because they were sinless, they didn't notice that they were not wearing any clothes. Then Satan whispered to Eve to whisper to Adam to eat from the tree, which they both did, and God punished them by banishing them as well," he said as he ran out of breath.

"Aha! Let's examine all these claims one by one. First, if God planned for Adam and Eve to be on earth in the first place, then all the events that took place after creating him and sending him to earth were also part of that plan, right?" I asked.

"I suppose so," he answered.

"Good. Now, according to the Quran, when God told the angels that He plans to create Adam, what was their response?"

"In the Quran, they asked God why He planned to create someone that will spread mischief on earth and shed blood."

"And how do they know that Adam and his species were going to spill blood and wreak havoc on earth?"

"Not sure. That's a great question."

"We don't have a definitive answer in the Quran, but the scholars have propounded remarkable theories about how *jinn* used to roam the earth and how they fought wars, etc. and the angels had their share of exposure to that, so they assumed Adam would do the same. Why doesn't this make a lot of sense?"

"That's easy. Why would the angels assume that Adam and his progeny would commit those crimes that were committed by an entirely different species? It wouldn't be a fair assumption about humans."

"Thank you. My thoughts exactly. So what is the only plausible explanation to the angels' question?"

"That…they have prior knowledge of human behaviour?" he said with great hesitation.

"Couldn't have put it better. We'll call this Exhibit A."

"Okay."

"Second, when God asked the angels to bow to Adam, all of them bowed except Satan, right?"

"Aha," he responded warily.

"What does that mean?"

"Not following."

"If I said all my students raised their hands except Abdullah, then you can automatically assume that Abdullah is…what?"

"Your student as well."

"Exactly. So, was Satan an angel?"

"Uhm…I don't think so. The Quran says he was from the *jinn* but disobeyed his Lord."

"Aha! So he was a *jinn*, yet is included with the bigger circle of angels. Why?"

"I don't know."

"The word *jinn* in Arabic means something that is hidden from the eyes. Is it possible that it pertains to all beings that are not seen, and lie beyond human perception?"

"Possible, yes."

"And if that's the case, then both angels and Satan would be considered what?"

"*Jinn*?"

"Quite possible, right?"

"Yes. Possible."

"Okay. Moving on. When God banished Satan from the Garden, and I call it a garden for a reason, what happened after?" I asked.

"Uhm, well, they roamed the garden, and Satan whispered to them," he answered.

"Wait. If God banished Satan and cursed him for eternity, what is he doing bothering the dwellers of heaven? If that Garden, called *Jannah* in the Quran, was the Garden of Eden, Paradise itself, then Satan would have accessed it?"

"Probably not."

"Which implies what?"

"Not sure…" he said with hesitation.

"Think about it. The words *jinn*, and *Jannah*, are derivatives of the same root word in Arabic, meaning something hidden from the eyes. Is it possible that *Jannah* was just a well-fortified Garden?" I asked him carefully.

"You mean…like a garden.. here on earth?" he answered with dismay.

"Yes, like a garden here on earth!"

"But…that's not what what I —"

I interrupted him and blurted, "Grew up with?"

"Yes!"

"Like I said, if I said anything illogical stop me."

"Okay..."

"So if we knew that God banished Satan for his disobedience and insolence, and if we knew that God won't allow Satan to enter paradise, then it's more plausible that the *Jannah* referenced was actually a beautiful garden on earth."

"Right."

"I'll call that exhibit B," I said assertively.

"Okay."

"Third, the Quran says that when Adam sinned and ate from the tree, he was very remorseful and God granted him the very words of repentance that he needed to use, right?"

"Yes."

"Which again means that the whole thing was foreknown by the Creator, no?"

"Indeed it was."

"Very good. This will be exhibit C. Fourth, your nephew said that the fossil record shows that we've been around how many years?"

"Over 190,000 years for us Homo sapiens."

"Here's the thing. The Quran never makes mention of how long ago Adam, or any other prophet, walked the earth. But it's implausible that he existed that long ago, isn't it?"

"I suppose. Definitely not 200,000 years ago. That wouldn't make sense."

"Great. That will make exhibit D."

"Okay."

"So let's examine the picture we have here, and the exhibits we've generated. God had a plan to create Adam and Eve and intended for them to be on earth. Angels had prior knowledge of humans acting in violent and brutal ways. Satan's deception to Adam was foreknown by God and also part of His plan. Adam and Eve roamed a garden that is unlikely to be Paradise. Fossil records suggest that humans lived on earth a lot longer than Adam did. What conclusions can we reach here?"

"Not sure…or maybe I wouldn't dare say."

"Seriously! What comes to mind when we consider all these premises?" I pressed him.

"Well, I feel blasphemous saying it, but here goes: that Adam was not the first human, and that the Garden was actually on earth! There, I said it!"

I laughed amusedly and said, "Spot on my friend!"

"But how can this be true when no one ever talked about it before among the scholars?"

"Actually medieval theologian Ibn ul-Qayyim mentioned it briefly, and the Egyptian philosopher Dr. Abdul-Sabur Shahin spoke about it in one of his books."

"Never heard of that."

"Let's think about this out loud. Humanity existed for 200,000 years. They were mostly savages that spilled blood and hurt each other. Human self-consciousness and free will didn't exist in the form we understand them today. The angels were a witness to this entire species that excelled at spreading mischief on earth. Suddenly, God informs them of His plan to appoint one of them as His trustee."

"Appoint? Not create?" he interrupted me.

"Yes! Appoint. That's the word that is used in the Quran.[9] So obviously the angels were surprised, based on their prior knowledge of humans. But God tells them that He knows what they know not. It was at that point, that God took a member of that pre-existing human community and endowed him with free-will, self-consciousness and a moral sense. Man was born that day, conceptually and spiritually, although he physically existed from before. God wanted to get the newly appointed trustee ready for his battle on earth, so He kept him in this confined place called the Garden, which served as his training ground, or his bootcamp, so to speak."

"But what was Adam being trained for?" he asked with confusion.

"Great question. The Quran says that God taught Adam the "names" of all things. The scholars said that God taught Adam by way of inspiration and intuition the knowledge that is needed for him to not only survive on earth, but to build a moral civilisation and fulfil the trusteeship of God. All the basic stuff, from planting a seed through herding livestock, to simple math etc. was perhaps taught in the Garden. So it was in that Garden that Adam and Eve stayed for a while for their training to be completed. But there was one final test that Adam needed to pass before he was ready to go."

"And what was that?" he asked.

"The test of creativity and innovation. The test of problem solving. The test of leadership and civilisation building. Adam can't just be a self-aware being with enough knowledge of the world. He needed to be ready to improvise, to adapt and to come up with solutions for his changing environment and evolving challenges. And for that, ironically, Adam needed to learn how to break from norms, how to go against the grain and how to think outside the box. And for that task, God brought another piece into the chessboard."

"Satan!" he screamed.

"Yes! Satan. His role was to push Adam to the limit. To expose him to his own weaknesses and strengths. To teach Adam that he's both vulnerable and invincible. To show him the path to spiritual freedom through repentance, but most importantly, to show him that the only way to build a civilisation on earth and to truly be the best representative of God's interest is to possess an independent voice. When he dares to rebel. When he takes risks. After all, law-abiding citizens who follow existing norms, and abide by all laws can be the gears in an engine, but can't be the force that steers the vehicle."

"Wait…you're not saying what I think you are, are you?"

"What do you think I'm saying?" I asked with a big smile.

"That God wanted Adam to disobey!"

"Not entirely. God was waiting for Adam to be ready, and his ability to disobey was the sign that he was!"

"This is…well…"

"Crazy?" I interrupted.

"Yes!"

"Well, it might be. But it's where I stand. Adam's disobedience was a telling moment that he had the qualities needed to lead. As long as that disobedience is followed by repentance. God was not looking for a loose-canon, foolhardy, out-of-control rebel either. Just someone who had the quality of thinking for himself and using his own free will. Adam still repented and became a prophet to his own people and his family, because he was able to find that balance."

"Does that mean Adam didn't descend from heaven to earth?"

"Yes. He didn't. It makes more sense that way because when you look at the Quran in general, God repeatedly says that Adam is created from the mud of the earth, right?"

"Yes, he does."

"When you compare the main ingredients of man, and that of the earth, you'll realise we're made of the same stuff: water, minerals etc. with almost the same ratios."

"I see. Forgive me for being in disbelief. This whole thing is new to me. Can any of this be supported by the Quran?"

"That's the best part!" I said in jubilation.

"How?"

"Examine the verses. In one verse, God says: "We created man from sounding clay, from mud molded into shape. And the *jinn* race, We had created before, from the fire of a scorching wind. Behold! Your Lord said to the angels: I am about to create man, from sounding clay from mud molded into shape!"[10]

"Yes. I'm familiar with the verses."

"Great. What is the order here?"

"First, God created *jinn*, then He created man, then He created Adam…Oh my God! I see it now!"

"What do you see?"

"The order. God is saying that He created *jinn* first, which is all the unseen beings, then He says that man in general, as in Homo sapiens, was created second, and then God created Adam by selecting one of those existing men!"

"Couldn't have put it better," I said calmly.

"This is fascinating…any other Quranic references?" he asked impatiently.

"In another *surah*, God says: "God did choose Adam and Noah, the family of Ibrahim and the family of Imran above all people."[11] When I say someone was chosen, what does that mean to us?"

"That there were others to choose from!"

"Indeed. It's almost as if God is saying there were other men but I chose and selected Adam for the task."

"This is becoming more interesting!"

"In another verse, God says about Adam: "Thereafter, His Lord elected him, accepted his repentance, and bestowed His guidance upon him,"[12] indicating that again, Adam was chosen from amongst others, to be endowed with consciousness, self-awareness, and divine forgiveness."

"It's almost as if I'm hearing those verses for the first time!" he said with amazement.

"I know. But here's another example. In the Quran, God also talks about how He created humans, and shaped them into what they are, and *then* asked the angels to prostrate to Adam.[13] The creation part comes in the plural, but the prostration part comes in the singular, just about Adam, again, implying that there is a possible process of creation that brought humans beings to existence, before Adam became who he was and the angels were asked to prostrate to him."

"Fascinating! But I still have a question. The story of Adam also includes what happened between Cain and Abel. If that was considered the first murder, then how is it that the angels witnessed mankind shed blood before?" he asked.

"Prior to Adam receiving the gift of self-awareness and moral consciousness from God, taking a life was not murder, unless you considered a lion killing a deer to be murder."

"Oh wow! So what humans did prior to Adam was just considered animal behaviour?"

"There you have it."

"Wow! But what about the wording in the Quran as it addresses the expulsion of Adam from the Garden? It uses the word 'descend'[14] and not 'leave'. What do we make of this?" he asked with great curiosity.

"Well, that leaving the sublime place that is the Garden constitutes a tremendous downgrade that it can be described as descension. This same meaning was alluded to by the great Quran commentator of the 20th century Imam Rashid Rida."

"This is incredible."

"You see, once we've looked at creation in those terms, we can conclude that the evolutionary process does exist, and it's driven by the power and might of the Creator. Thinking of the creation of man as the bringing-to-self-consciousness of a being that already existed physically and endowing him with morality and self-awareness, is the most logical way to still reconcile evolution with creation," I said confidently.

"My life has changed forever," he said while shaking his head in disbelief.

"For the better I hope," I said confidently.

"So the Adamic Intellectual Endowment paradigm leaves no incompatibility between evolution and faith. One can fully believe in God and accept the science of evolution without question. This is amazing! My nephew's mind will be blown away!"

"Always excited about our discussions and praying for you and your nephew."

"Thank you Imam! You're a blessing."

"Just pray for my family."

"You don't have to ask!"

He greeted me and walked out of my door. I smiled, as I looked at my *khutba* notes, took a deep breath, and put ink back to paper.

*Chapter 7*

# Reason

I was darting through the aisles of the grocery store, scanning a list of items my wife asked me to purchase, while listening to one of my favourite audiobooks. He suddenly showed up pushing another cart at the end of the aisle. He looked at me and quickly a big smile found its way to his face, and mine. It's almost like he was amused to see the Imam personally doing shopping for his family. He moved toward me with his big smile.

"Assalamu'alaikum Imam!" he said to me with unusually bright eyes.

"Wa alaykum assalam! Long time no see. How's the family?" I answered earnestly.

"Everyone is well, thank you for asking."

"What's the latest and greatest about your nephew?"

"Still struggling, but signs of hope abound!"

"Happy to hear! Have you guys been meeting and talking?"

"Yes, plenty of meetings and many conversations. He seems to be interested in having these intellectual discussions. Thanks to you I have a lot to share now! Oh, and by the way, I noticed that he still has your keychain gift on him. There are no keys on it, but I saw it in his hands. He keeps taking it out of his pocket, playing with it nervously, and putting it back!"

I smiled silently.

"It's a start *alhamdulillah*," he said.

"This is heartwarming. Just be aware that the purpose of those conversations should not be to defeat him intellectually, or even to bring him back to Islam," I said firmly.

"Then what is the purpose?" he asked.

"To have an honest dialogue about God and the universe. At the end of the day everyone has a journey that they have to take. We can only pray, but guidance is a mere gift from the Creator to those who open their hearts and minds to it."

"Do you think my nephew is one of them?"

"I don't think so. I believe so! Otherwise you guys wouldn't be having all those discussions. His heart is searching. Be there with answers if you can."

"I'm trying. He seems to be stuck on —"

"Excuse me!" another shopper interrupted him as she was moving with her cart through the aisle, wanting to pass us. At that moment I realised that I was having an existential conversation with a community member at the pasta aisle of a grocery store.

"So sorry!" I said to her. She passed us while scanning items on the shelves.

"Listen, if you're done shopping, should we check out?" I asked him.

"Absolutely. So sorry I got carried away," he said apologetically.

"No worries!"

I walked with him towards the check out line. Once we stood waiting for our turns, I asked him, "You were saying your nephew was stuck on what?"

"Ah yes, I was saying he's stuck on something we haven't discussed before."

"What is it?"

"He keeps ending every conversation with this statement that is filled with despair 'we're all stardust'. One day I asked him what that meant, and he said: it means all of us, everything around us, is just matter. We're all made of molecules and atoms and that's it. One day we all go back to the earth and get mixed up with dirt again. We become indistinguishable from rocks and mud."

"And how did you respond to this?"

"I would say stuff like: yes, sure, we're made of the same stuff and our bodies will go back to the earth, but we're not made of just matter. There's a soul, and spirit, and those will go back to God."

"And how does he respond to this?"

"Sometimes he shrugs, sometimes he scoffs, and other times he gazes into the distance in rumination."

"I see."

"How can we address this? This whole thing about us being made of matter, and the soul cannot be proven?" he asked.

"Ah…the good ol' naturalism argument. Got to get me some of that!" I said sarcastically.

"I'm serious!"

"Me too! See, deep inside, I believe that many modern day prophets of atheism are angry. At God, at family, at an unjust world, you name it. Instead of finding ways to reconcile and cope, they turn the world into a place darker than their own thoughts."

"In a way I actually agree, judging by what this whole thing did to my nephew. But what does that have to do with stardust?"

"Let me walk you through this one. I need your attention!"

"When have I ever not granted it?" he said with a wink.

"Touché!"

He chuckled.

"Next!" the cash register clerk said loudly. I started putting my items on the belt, as I continued my conversation with him.

"Okay. So essentially, atheists who claim to hinge their arguments upon scientific foundations, tend to consider themselves philosophic naturalists," I said.

"What's naturalism?"

"See, methodological naturalism is a statement about the scope of science, where it is argued, and quite convincingly, that science is done through observation, and without any reference to metaphysics and supernatural causes. Science, in this view, is entirely sufficient to explain natural phenomena and events without having to resort to explanation in religion. On the other hand, a philosophic naturalist is someone who believes this entire universe, our earth, and all of its living beings including us, are exclusively made of the same stuff, which is atoms and molecules only. We're all composed of particles that came from the stars, in the sense that when stars explode as supernovas, their fragments, pieces, and particles travel across the universe. And since our solar system originated from such particles, it follows, in the atheist dark drama, that we're all made of that same "stardust". This applies to our physical bodies, but also our thoughts, ideas, memories, feelings, etc. There's no other component to the human being. There's no soul, and there's no spirit. Just nerve impulses and base desires, all made of sodium, potassium, iron, zinc, carbon etc. There's no moral code or a sense of right and wrong. Even emotions or love or patriotism, are all nerve impulses designed for the purpose of survival. We do what we do because we are determined to do so in our genetic coding. It's all nature and nothing is nurture. The universe just is. It has no purpose, no direction, and no meaning. It's just there because its building components made it so."

"Well...this is the most depressing thing I've ever heard," he said with a sombre look.

"I don't disagree," I said as I was using my credit card to pay.

"If this were true though, it would be a very cruel existence."

"Indeed. Imagine a universe where there is no such thing as good and evil. It's just lawful and unlawful, legal and illegal, beneficial and harmful etc. Imagine the consequences of this thinking. Crimes are not bad anymore. They're just acts of people who are genetically determined, fatalistically, to be how they are. A child molester is not a bad person. He's just who he is. It's not his fault that he sees little kids as objects of pleasure. The actions of an older man preying on the flesh of a little girl are no more ethically reprehensible than a lion preying on a gazelle. They're just doing what they're biologically determined to do. It's how their "stardust" arrangement led them to be. There's no escape," I said, as I moved away with my cart, waiting for him to check out.

"This is absolutely depressing. Sounds more like religious fatalism and predetermination!" he said.

"Actually a lot worse. At least *qadr* can change with prayer. Your genetics cannot."

"I can imagine all kinds of terrifying scenarios arising from this understanding," he said.

"Without a doubt. If all that happens to us after death is that we disintegrate into the earth and our molecules are rearranged, then what's the point of living, abiding by laws and morals, or respecting life? In such a bleak existence, the question is not whether we should just commit suicide or even murder others, rather, why shouldn't we?"

"They will say because the person you murder has loved ones that will cry when we take his life!"

"To which naturalists must say: love, just like all other human emotions, is just arbitrary nerve impulses running through our nerves in ways that aid survival. It has no real meaning or value beyond that. The siblings of a gazelle may feel the 'sadness' of losing her but the lion still doesn't, or perhaps shouldn't feel bad after eating her."

"But still, we're not animals. Taking a life hurts human society in other ways and leaves us all in jeopardy," he said urgently, as he pushed his cart forward, and we both walked towards the exit of the store.

"Actually it only leaves in jeopardy those who are not willing to kill for what they need and want. But those who are willing to, will emerge higher and more advantageous," I responded.

"But this is why we have laws, right?"

We both walked in the parking lot towards my car, as I answered.

"Sure, arbitrary laws that are designed to lessen the impact of this horrific chaos. But those laws hinge upon no notion of right or wrong. Just slowing down the path of destruction. Legality without morality is an arbitrary line between identical types of behaviour.

There is no more black-and-white separation between what is good and what is not. Just a random line that society arbitrarily drew. Otherwise, legal and illegal behaviour, if naturalists are right, are inherently identical."

"Lord…this is terrifying," he said with a broken voice. At that point, we had already arrived at my car, so I stopped my cart next to the car and responded.

"It sure is. Racism, sexism, misogyny, slavery, and all abominable human tendencies are not evil according to this understanding. They just are what they are. There is no such thing as human rights in a moral sense. Just what we design arbitrarily under the weight of political pressure or the trauma of war."

"Extremely disturbing."

"It is. And it gets worse when we think about happiness or purpose. In a naturalist world, true happiness cannot be attained. We can only be truly happy as a result of the self-actualisation that is inherent in our ability to understand our purpose and fulfil our mission in this life. Without purpose, there can be no true happiness."

"But people can still feel happy. Through food, sex, economic success etc. Someone will claim that as a naturalist they still experience happiness, right?" he asked with hesitation.

"Wrong. This would not be happiness. It would be a distraction. It's like putting someone in a really fancy jail and telling him listen, we're going to shower you with food, women, and the fancy things in life, as long as you don't ask why you are here and when you'll be released, and what's out there in the world. This is not happiness. Just a way to keep someone's mind off the real question, the answer to which will grant true happiness. This question is simple, and it goes like this: what is my purpose?" I said firmly.

"But what if someone said it's okay, if we don't have a purpose let's work together on creating one for ourselves?"

"I would say it still doesn't work. It's like saying: we don't have a purpose so let's just pretend to have one. If there's no end goal to our existence, any so-called purpose is just fun and games. It's not real. A purpose is something that we realise and discover, not manufacture. It precedes me and exists before I come to existence. I'm here to fulfil it. If we create purpose then we have no purpose. We can only create goals, but multiple goals must serve a higher purpose that we do not choose."

"This makes sense. But naturalists might concede to all these arguments and say: you're absolutely right, and we're sorry that the universe is like this, purposeless and hopeless. We don't like it either, and we wish it were different. But this is how it is, and there's nothing we can do about it."

"I'd say they're wrong. The universe is NOT like this. We don't behave like purposeless animals. We do feel that sense of purpose deep in our bones. We fight our predispositions all the time in order to serve that goal. Most of us know that there's something inherently wrong about taking an innocent life or sexually exploiting children, including those who are inclined to act that way. We make sacrifices all the time in order to serve the ones we love. Sacrifices that come at our own expense more often than not. And surprisingly to naturalists, we still feel genuine happiness when we do. We cooperate with others, we serve others, and protect others, not because of what the law says, but because of an innate sense of right and wrong. Even in societies where certain unbecoming behaviour has become acceptable, many still refrain from it because of that sense of morality. Without the police breathing down your neck, you might still find a satchel full of cash and refrain from taking the money, against your desire. This doesn't look like the genetically fatalistic world naturalists would have us believe in," I said.

"I will make sure to share this perspective with my nephew. What's fascinating is that atheists always use the word reason to support all of their arguments. But once you examine those arguments you realise they fall flat on their faces and defy reason," he responded, while shaking his head.

"Great point, and that's why they're really dangerous when they disguise their arguments with pseudo rationality. But here's the thing, even reason as a concept can be used against naturalism, and not in its favour, and this is not just about their arguments proving to be unreasonable."

"What do you mean?"

"What I mean is reason as an intellectual faculty. It precedes knowledge; it precedes science and observation."

"What do you mean precedes?"

"Reason is an ability of our minds that exists innately therein. It's a faculty of processing multifold perceptions and grouping them into meaningful thought. It doesn't exist in the natural world. It doesn't need observation of any physical reality to come to being."

"I still don't understand," he said with a confused voice.

"Let me use an example. Here's a simple deductive argument: all animals that live underwater are marine animals. An octopus lives underwater, therefore?"

"Uhm…an octopus is a marine animal?"

"Exactly! Let me ask you: the statement you just made right now, is that a statement of science or reason?"

"I'm not sure."

"If it were a statement of science, then it needs to be based on what?" I asked patiently.

"Observation?"

"Indeed. Did you observe all marine life and come to that conclusion?"

"No."

"Then this type of deductive thinking is what?"

"A matter of reason I guess."

"It definitely is. Let me use another example to make my point clear. Every balooza you observed today is pink, can we deduct that at least some baloozas are pink?"

"What on earth is a balooza?"

"Don't worry about that now. Is the argument and its conclusion valid?"

"That some baloozas are pink?"

"Yes."

"Well, if someone observed the, uhm, baloozas, and they were pink, then yes, at least some of them are pink."

"Without having to see every balooza in the world?"

"There would be no need to examine all the baloozas. I've already seen some that are pink and that's enough."

"Have you seen a balooza?" I asked with a chuckle.

"No!"

"So, what is a balooza?"

"I have no idea."

"That's my point right there. Without ever seeing this balooza, your mind used deductive reasoning to reach a conclusion."

"I see that. But what's a balooza?"

"It doesn't exist. It's a made-up thing. I just used it to show you that deductive reasoning is a conceptual process that is not based on the empirical data of the observable world. It's not a matter of science. Just rationality."

"Interesting example, but I do get your point now. What do we learn from this?" he asked curiously.

"A whole lot! Reason is a process only of the human mind. It's not dependent on physical reality or sense perception. It's 'a priori'. As a matter of fact, scientists and naturalists would just assume its existence if the observations of physical reality are to be processed and made sense of. Reason cannot be proven by science because it is assumed by science as a necessary condition for any scientific endeavour and inquiry."

"It just resides in our minds," he affirmed.

"Yes. It does. But here's the kicker. Naturalists argue that the entire universe is made of molecules and particles. No purpose, no reason, no rationale. Just arrangements of molecules. This includes us, and by consequence it includes our brains, and our sense of reason, right?"

"I suppose so. In order for naturalists to be consistent, they have to concede that our brains are made of the same stuff."

"Agreed. Tell me then: if we are made of 'stuff' that has no reason or purpose, how did our brains develop the capacity to reason and have a purpose? If we are just a rearrangement of arbitrary particles that have absolutely no sense of reason, how come the end product of that rearrangement does possess the ability to reason?" I asked.

"Fascinating question! It would not make sense of course. In a universe where there is no God, everything arises from the physical world in a non-rational process and without reason. If this is true, then nothing rational should come of it!" he said.

"Not only that, if it is true that the entire universe lacks purpose or reason, and that by extension since we belong to the universe and are made of the same stuff, our minds, thoughts, and ideas also lack purpose or reason, then all human intellectual constructs or truth claims are essentially arational, if not outright irrational, and lack reason, and this would include the atheist/naturalist narrative as well! In other words, the conclusion to a naturalist argument is that naturalism -and of course any other human thought process- is irrational!"

"Total mic drop there!" he said with a chuckle.

"The intention is not to defeat anything or put down any idea. Rather, to use this incredible faculty, that despite what naturalists would have us believe, we actually do possess: reason!"

"So it's either naturalism is true, in which case its conclusions would likely be irrational, or naturalism is wrong, in which case its conclusions are definitely irrational!"

"Couldn't have put it better! As atheists filled our heads with false arguments against God, claiming that divinity is a concept that cannot be proven by science, they use another concept that cannot be proven by science, which is reason, in order to establish the validity of every scientific claim they've ever made. It's remarkable," I said with a tone of irony.

"It absolutely is. But let me be the devil's advocate and ask this: what if the ability to reason evolved in human beings over millennia in order for us to be able to survive? Would this save the naturalist argument?"

"Who said that reason is a necessary condition for survival? Frogs, ants, and protozoa survive just fine without reason. In fact, sometimes superstitious, unreasonable fears, guarantee better chances of survival."

"How come?"

"Think about it. Someone who believes in horoscopes, and decides not to go out when it's raining, or on Tuesdays, or on Friday the 13th, or whatever, and tends to worry about being in places or interacting with people, for totally superstitious reasons, that person ends up driving less, and meeting fewer people, and therefore becomes less subject to possible car accidents, infections, etc. Someone, for irrational reasons, decided to avoid all fungi for fear of poisoning. That person would end up not eating any fungi, including non-poisonous mushrooms, but also become less liable for poisonous fungi. Wouldn't all that make the lack of reason, sometimes, better for survival?"

"There's a smackdown!" he said with excitement.

"Observing human behaviour, you actually realise that we behave entirely opposite to the naturalist/survivalist narrative. We have an innate desire to explore. We sometimes put ourselves in harm's way to learn more, to find more and discover more, sometimes at our own peril. We desire glory, recognition, and fame. We take risks, explore outer space and engage in activities that may sometimes lead to the opposite of survival actually. We use our reason as we please, and put it on hold when we need to. Reason can be calculating and ominous, and pure sentimentalism can bring us more happiness occasionally. This is what makes us human. There's nothing genetically predetermined here."

"This is astounding!"

"You're welcome," I said with a smile.

"But here's another possible refutation. Computers are made of metal that lacks any reason, yet they're capable of thinking and using reason. How do we respond to this?"

I laughed out loud, and my laugh infected him, so he laughed as well.

"I'm serious," he said with urgency.

"Computers don't think, my friend. We endowed them with the ability to process equations, so they process equations. Unlike us, they don't 'know' what they're doing. They deliver results precisely as they have been programmed. They don't have reason or self-consciousness. Computers don't engage in abstract thought or produce original ideas. They don't write novels or compose sonatas. For example, water and oxygen come together and make water. Two gasses make a fluid. But both are physical entities and through the predictable equations of chemistry, the molecules interact with each other, in a process that leads to a change in the physical features of both components. We may alter the atoms and molecules of bananas and make oranges out of them in some kind of a high-profile lab experiment, but you sure cannot produce poetry out of a cake. You cannot produce something rational from something that lacks any rationality."

"What about artificial intelligence? AI computers can develop self-consciousness and make rational decisions on their own, independent of any input from the scientist that created them. They become self-aware so to speak, right?"

"No, they don't. They're still programmed, but their programming involves more decision-making liberties. To enable those devices to respond to situations that the maker didn't predict, their coding allows for some room to improvise if you will. But even then, at that moment when AI needs to 'decide', it does so based on parameters that are predetermined in its coding. AI computers cannot physically act like they do in the movies and build weapons to protect themselves. Self-preservation is a quality of the living. An AI machine will respond in a sophisticated way to complex problems and evolve to address increasing challenges and demands, but won't experience depression, or decide to get married to another AI or feel bored from working, and all the other qualities that are truly reflected in the notion of 'self-awareness' as we understand it as human beings."

"I think I'm totally satisfied, Imam," he said.

"Happy to hear."

"I have another question though, since we're still talking about reason."

"Please, by all means," I said assuredly.

"My nephew recently brought up one of his old arguments again. That science as the most reliable method of inquiry can be used to disprove, but not to prove God. How do I respond to this?"

"That science is not really reliable 100% of the time, and that it must never be used to either prove or disprove God!"

"Are you suggesting that science can be biased? This would be such a big statement though."

"I'm not saying it's biased. It's the best we've got. All I'm saying is that scientific research is still bound by culture, politics, and funding. Research, just like any other human endeavour, takes the path of least resistance."

"Does that make it unreliable?" he asked.

"I didn't say science was unreliable. This would be a transgression on my part. Without science we wouldn't be having this conversation. My point is that scientific endeavours, just like any other human institution, cannot be entirely isolated from subjective human perspectives. Science is a useful instrument. It's an indispensable device that answers our day-to-day questions, provides practical solutions to our problems, and makes our lives more convenient. Scientific advancements made it possible for us to fight disease, combat hunger, and explore outer space. On the other hand, honest scientists, and most reasonable people, never claim that science provides a comprehensive worldview that can replace culture, religion, and tradition. This would be scientism not science, and it would be rejected as a false ideology. Science, by definition, is limited and volatile. What we know today changes tomorrow. What is considered a fact today will be rendered obsolete in later times. Scientific observations must go through the never-ending processing of human subjectivity, from observational bias to lab testing, to politics, to funding, to popular culture etc. Is it still ultimately useful? Without a doubt. But when science is used as an ideological foundation to overrule established cultures, traditions, systems of thought, and feelings that it simply cannot explain, such as love, consciousness, and intuition, or reason for that matter, that is when its deployment becomes harmful."

"Interesting. Not sure if I fully agree. How else does science fall short?" he asked cynically.

"When we realise that science cannot provide definitive answers to moral and ethical challenges. It cannot instruct me on how to lead a virtuous life, raise my kids, feel satisfied, fulfil my family obligations, sacrifice for my family or my country, live an honourable life, have a sharp conscience etc."

"I appreciate this perspective. Hearing you speak though, made me feel as if science, in general, would point towards a direction of no God. Is that a safe assumption?"

"Absolutely not. Scientism may be, but not science. Many scientific truths point towards the direction of a creator."

"Like what? I know it'll come up in my nephew's conversations at one point or the other."

"Science and God may have taken a collision course and became mutually exclusive during the days of medieval Christian Europe, but such a clash didn't take place during the Muslim Golden Age for instance when science and God were considered perfectly compatible."

"Any examples? "

"Well, as I said in a previous conversation, take for instance mathematical constants that we discovered in the universe. Small g, Capital G, Pie, e etc. We see those constants in thermochemistry, physics, and biology. Who made those? And why are they so specific? You see?"

"I do."

"In my opinion, one of the greatest proofs of God in science lies in quantum physics," I said.

"Oh boy.... that complicated field again."

"It is complicated, but the way we talk about it as laymen can make it simple enough."

"How?"

"Quantum physics is the branch of science that studies the behaviour of subatomic particles, meaning particles that are as small as neutrons, electrons, quarks etc."

"Okay. Not as complicated."

"Quantum physicists have long marvelled at the fact that subatomic particles behave as both particles and waves interchangeably."

"Waves?"

"Yes, like light waves, radio waves, electromagnetic etc."

"Wait, doesn't being a particle necessarily mean it's not a wave?"

"Yes! And that's why physicists marvel at the concept."

"Wow!"

"Moreover, physicists cite the Heisenberg Uncertainty Concept, where the behaviour of those subatomic particles is actually determined by the observer. I think we spoke about this a few weeks ago."

"I remember you talking about this before, but can you refresh my memory? What do you mean the observer?" he asked.

"I mean the physicist that is making the observation, pertaining to the location of a given particle, or its behaviour as mass or wave."

"Are you saying that the observer affects the behaviour of the particle?"

"True. This is one of the most incredible findings of quantum physics that sets it completely apart from conventional physics, where the observer is neutral. In quantum physics, the observer is actually a participant!"

"While this is very complex, from the little I understood, it sounds astounding!"

"I know. Without the observer, physicists say, the only thing we know about a particle is its existence in time and space. Only when the observer is participating do we know where it is and its potential behaviour. And this changes every time the observer changes."

His eyes were just wide open with astonishment. "But what does all this tell us about the universe and God?" he asked.

"Well, for starters it tells us that the observer is not just a neutral spectator, but an active participant in shaping reality. It also demonstrates so much through the concept of nonlocality."

"What is that?"

"It's a concept of quantum physics, where quantum particles can influence each other and interact with each other without necessarily making any contact, as opposed to the assumptions of conventional physics. Imagine how this can change the way we think of the universe, which is made of those near-infinite quantum particles! Imagine how interconnected the entire universe is, and how all its particulars are literally 'communicating' with each other."

"And of course all of this lends itself to the unity of the universe, and that supports a Designer as opposed to random chance!" he said with great amazement.

"Without any doubt. It also might shed some light to explain phenomena that conventional sciences fail to explain, such as feelings, self-consciousness, prayer, telepathy, cellular memory etc." I said.

"What's cellular memory?" he asked.

"The observation that cells may have memories of their own, that demonstrates itself when they are transplanted to someone else."

"How?!" he said with a panicked voice.

"Well, there has been a plethora of evidence that people who underwent organ transplant have retained certain intimate memories of the donor that may have passed on to them through the transplanted organ."

"This is utterly insane!"

"Not if you employ the tools of quantum physics to understand them."

"Wow."

"Last but not least is the concept of fractals," I added.

"The concept of what?"

"Fractals."

"What is that exactly?"

"Fractals are mathematical patterns that exist in nature at both the macro and microscopic levels, in which its different layers are similar in shape as you zoom in and out."

"Still don't get it."

"To make a complex concept simple, think of the tree shape. What is it made of?"

"Trunk, branches, leaves etc."

"Great! Now think of yourself as a giant who's bigger than the entire universe looking on to it. Science has proven that galaxies are organised in clusters that are like trees. Trunk, branches, sub-branches etc."

"Okay, I'm following."

"Now imagine that you as a giant were given this magical telescope that allows you to zoom in further and further into the universe."

"Okay. Weird, but okay," he said with a chuckle.

"As you zoom in, you realise that the tree shape with its branches and sub-branches exists at every layer of magnification. At the level of solar systems and how they're distributed within the galaxy, to the level of earth and how rivers meander and branch out, onto the level of coastlines and actual trees, to snowflakes and branching blood vessels, and the motion of molecules at the microscopic levels. They all follow the same geometric patterns."

"I feel so bad being so ignorant of all this!"

"Fractals tell us a lot about the unity of the universe's creation, and how order and design exist in what atheists see as pure chaos."

"This was extremely heartwarming, Imam. Dare I ask how you know all this?"

"I'm a student of knowledge. I take both pride and comfort in my journey as I navigate through the Lord's dominion and expose myself to the wonders of His creation."

"May God keep our hearts strong and inspired."

"Ameen."

"Okay, so sorry I took too much of your time," he said apologetically.

"No worries at all. I rather enjoyed it!"

"I need to schedule a meeting with my nephew right away," he said.

"Best of luck!"

"So sorry to have kept you in the parking lot for so long on such a cold day! Let me help you out with your stuff!" he said.

"Sure!" I said as I opened the trunk. He started making room by moving items around. He picked up a book titled *The Ethics* by Spinoza, held it in his hand, shook his head, looked at me, and said with a laugh, "How many Imams carry philosophy books in their trunks?"

"Well, you only carry weapons if you think you're involved in a battle," I said with a shy smile.

"Man. You're such a rarity," he said.

"In a good way, I hope," I said as I was putting the rest of the items in the car. When everything was safely tucked in, he closed the trunk, turned to me, and said, "Please keep me and my nephew in your prayers!"

"I will, inshaAllah."

He marched away, and I walked towards the driver's door, sat down in my driver's seat, paused for a moment to take a deep breath, resumed playing my audiobook on Voltaire, and drove away.

*Chapter 8*

# Destiny

He walked towards me after Friday prayer and approached with a serious look.

"Dear Imam, I have some updates," he said.

"Always happy to hear your updates. Is it about your nephew?" I asked.

"Who else is it going to be about?" he responded with a sigh.

"Updates are good, right?"

"In a way. Our conversations are progressing. I'm learning so much through my dialogue with him. This experience helped me dig deeper into my own faith and reshape my worldview. I realised how shallow I've always been. And how insubstantial my commitment to God was."

I looked at him with supportive eyes without saying anything.

"But my nephew still has some serious questions that I couldn't answer," he continued.

"Like what?"

"He cornered me the other day and challenged my perceptions of God as the Lord that manages our affairs and answers our prayers."

"What's wrong with that?" I asked curiously.

"He says it defies free will."

"It's ironic because naturalists don't believe in free will," I said dismissively.

"I told him that, and he said he's pointing out the inconsistency in religious discourse."

"Why does he see an inconsistency?"

"Well, because telling someone that God determines all their choices, but at the same time they have freewill, is confusing and demoralising, he says, and I agree with him."

"I see. So you assume that this is the Islamic position on the topic?"

"If it is not, then we did a pretty bad job educating Muslims about it! Most people assume this entire subject is confusing and makes no sense. Some are able to live with the inconsistency and others just leave the faith because of it," he said with frustration.

"Okay. Can you share with me some of the questions that folks bring up?"

"Well, I don't know where to start. They ask questions like: what is the meaning of qada (decree) and Qadr (destiny)? What's the difference between them? Are they the same as fatalism and predestination? Does God determine our future choices or does He just know about them? If He determines them, how can we still have free will? And if He only knows about the future, then what's the point of us doing anything or making any choices when it's already foreknown by God? Doesn't that mean if I choose to sit at home and do nothing then God already knows about it? What's the point of praying and making dua if the course is already set? And if God 'answers' our prayers, does that mean it is what was going to happen anyway, in which case why pray in the first place? Does God guide whoever He wills and misguide whomever He wills? And what does that say about my fate and personal choice? If one's age is determined already, then why stay healthy or exercise, since it won't make a difference anyway? If one's rizq (sustenance) is already determined, then what's the point of effort and hard work? Is it true that people will be in heaven forever? What will they do? Won't they get bored? If everything is determined, can we say that evil people are not responsible for their actions? And why does God allow evil to exist in the world in the first place if He's such a loving God? Why does He allow children to suffer and die? Why do bad things happen to good people? What is luck and chance? And where do they fit in the *qada* and *qadr* theology? And I can say more!"

"Good grief," I said with a sense of shock.

"I know! Sorry to dump all this on you at once, but it's pretty serious like I said. My nephew is still struggling with these questions and my generic responses are not working!"

"I understand. Let me walk you through this step by step".

"Can't wait!"

"The Quran states clearly that the knowledge we already possess is very limited, no?"

"Yes. God says: "You have been granted very little real knowledge."[15]

"Exactly. The example I like to use is that of a fish tank. My brother has one. Every time I look at it, I can't help but think that those fish keep swimming all day long in their very limited reality. They think the entire universe lies within the walls of that fish tank. They know nothing about what happens outside. They can only understand water, crumbs, mating, eating each other maybe, but nothing more. They possess some knowledge for sure, but it's very limited knowledge, wouldn't you agree?" I asked.

"Yes. They only know what their small brains can process," he answered.

"Precisely. Fish in a tank cannot possibly fathom anything beyond the tank. They don't understand the laws of gravity, the Arab-Israeli conflict or culinary arts! Does it make sense?"

"Perhaps…but what does that have to do with our discussion?"

"My point is: what if we are fish in a tank? Our perception of reality is not only restricted by our technological limitations, but most importantly by the intellectual boundaries of our primitive minds. That is simply insurmountable."

"I have to agree there."

"Now, based on that, can we say that we can only understand reality using the language of our limited, four-dimensional universe?" I asked.

"Well, based on String Theory, our universe is 11-dimensional, but yes, I see your point. We can only perceive the four dimensions in our 4D-animated world: length, width, breadth and time," he responded.

"Absolutely! Now let me ask you: if we believe in God, would we say that He belongs to the 4D universe and suffers from its limitations?"

"Obviously not. We'd say He created it and cannot be limited by it."

"Great. So every time God wants to talk to us, with our limited 4D minds, what needs to happen?"

"A process of translation of some sort I presume. In which complex notions from an infinitely-dimensional existence are communicated to minds that only understand a 4D existence, right?"

"Brilliant! Couldn't have put it better! The very words of the scriptures originated in infinite existence, must be "watered down" and diluted and perhaps completely transformed to be contained within the boundaries of limited human language to express God's will in a comprehensible way!" I said.

"That's a fair point. But I still cannot make the connection."

"What I mean to say here is that concepts such as time, future, choice, good, evil, freedom etc. are very strictly human in the sense that they only operate within a material, contingent, and caused 4D world."

"I think that would make sense. But what are the consequences of this understanding?" he asked.

"I will get to that, but let's first examine a few things."

"Sure."

"First, every ounce of knowledge in our minds, collectively, belongs to this limited 4D universe. History, language, philosophy, logic etc. are all 4D, right?"

"I suppose."

"Second, any knowledge that exists beyond our 4D perception

can only be processed after some 'treatment' to make it comprehensible, right?"

"Sure. We've already established that."

"What is the word that Islamic theology gives that knowledge beyond our perception?"

"*Ilm ul-Ghayb* I think?"

"That's it! Literally 'knowledge beyond our perception'. I don't see *Ilm ul-Ghayb* as believing in fairytales as atheists suggest, but a humble acceptance that what lies beyond my perception is simply larger than anything I can feel and process. I'm just a fish that can accept, with its limited intelligence, that there's a lot more that exists beyond the fish tank."

"That's fair. In the beginning of the second chapter of the Quran, God says, describing the qualities of true believers: 'those who believe in the knowledge beyond human perception'[16]," he said.

"Yes! Doesn't this mean that the words God uses to describe what happens in the realm of the unseen, must be understood based on where they originated?"

"Can you elaborate?" he asked.

"When God says 'pen' or 'book' or 'fire' or 'throne' etc. should it imply what those objects mean for us here, or what they mean for God?"

"For God I guess?"

"I would say so. So we have to take those notions with a grain of salt and be open to what they could possibly mean, and not just what we think they mean."

"I can live with that."

"Great. Now let us talk about time. After the renaissance, many scientists actually believed that the universe was beginningless, and therefore, eternal. This notion in and of itself could have completely dismantled the concept of God. If the universe had neither a beginning nor an end, then who needs a god? Charles Pierce was the first modern philosopher to dismiss the possibility of an eternal universe. Of course, he was preceded by Muslim and Greek philosophers who said the same. But as the Big Bang became the most popular and scientifically acceptable theory to explain the origin of the universe, we now know that the universe actually has a beginning, and will consequently have an end."

"Even someone who knows very little physics heard about all this," he said.

"Great. But here's the thing: 13.8 billion years ago, when the universe came into existence, it wasn't just 'space' that was synthesized, but 'time' as well," I said.

"What do you mean?"

"I mean prior to the Big-Bang, not only that there was no space as we understand it, -remember, there was no universe in the first place- but there was no time either! Time was a product of that event. Before it, our physical laws, reality as it were, did not exist."

"My head is spinning!"

"It will spin faster," I said with a chuckle.

He responded with a nervous grunt.

"What I'm trying to say here is that time is a creation, and all its derivatives, such as 'past', 'future', 'eternity', 'tomorrow', are very specific to our universe, bound by its physical laws and operate on objects that are created, caused and material. They are words that are being articulated in a 4D domain, describing a strictly 4D phenomenon, that is time."

"Okay. So what?"

"If time only belongs to our universe, is it or is it not true that anything that exists outside that universe doesn't experience time as we do, and therefore is not bound by its limitations?"

"I would say that it is true."

"Great. And since God is the Creator of the universe, and therefore is not bound by the limitations of our 4D universe, then what would logically follow?"

"That God is not bound by the limitations of time?"

"Exactly! He created it as part of His system. How can time be a boundary for Him when He brought it to existence?"

"It can't I suppose. But how can this help us understand fate and predestination?"

"It helps us understand a big part of it, but not all."

"How?"

"Pay attention to the questions you shared with me earlier. Does God know the future? Does God determine our future choices? Does God know in advance what we are going to do? Can my fate change if I prayed to God? How will people stay in heaven forever? etc."

"I don't get it."

"Look at the words that are being used: future, tomorrow, past, in advance, going to, change my fate, forever etc. What's common between these words?"

"The passage of time?"

"Yes! Thank you. The passage of time. Embedded in these questions is the erroneous assumption that on the one hand God created time and on the other hand subjects Himself to its physical limitations," I said.

"Still don't get it..sorry!"

"No need to apologise. Let me elaborate. When someone asks: does God know my 'future' choices? What does the question imply?"

"What?"

"That God experiences the passage of time the way we do!"

"Oh!"

"Yes! Which makes no sense. My brother created a fish tank, but it doesn't mean he has to breathe through gills! In order for an entity to be bound by time, this entity needs to be both material and caused. God is neither!"

"I think I'm beginning to see where you're going with this!"

"Great! Let me rephrase to make sure this is absolutely clear. God doesn't look at objects he created the way we do through the lens of time. There's no tomorrow or yesterday for Him. He doesn't experience the past, present or future. He exists outside the time-line. And once we remove the concept of time from the equation, suddenly things will look a lot clearer."

"How?" he asked.

"There will be no room for questions such as: does God know my 'future' choices, because He sees your entire life from begin-ning to end, all at once. He's not in the tank with you. For you, you can only see what happened and what's happening, but not what will happen. For God it's different. This understanding resolves questions about eternity in heaven, and getting bored there! There is no boredom because there is no passage of time! It addresses questions like: if God knows the future, then what's the point of doing anything? Once time is removed from divine consideration, the picture may not necessarily become perfectly clear, since we cannot fathom existence without time -remember, it's part of *Ilm ul-ghayb*- but it certainly becomes more plausible and less illog-ical," I said.

"I see. This is very interesting, but it might only resolve ques-tions about God's knowledge of our actions, but how can it address questions about God's intervention and predestination?"

"For that, we need a different type of inquiry."

"Great!"

"Here's the thing. I noticed over the years the Quran makes it unequivocally clear that human beings own their choices, and will be held accountable for those choices. I can think of so many verses in the scripture where this is unequivocally stated. For ex-ample: 'Man can have nothing but what he strives for, and that the fruit of his striving will soon come to sight'[17] or 'God guides unto Himself all those who turn unto Him'[18] or 'If anyone contends with the Messenger even after guidance has been plainly conveyed to him, and follows a path other than that becoming to men of faith, We shall leave him in the path he has chosen, and land him in Hell, what an evil refuge'[19] or 'Let him who wills believe in it and let him who wills reject it'.[20] All this indicates that humans are free to make what?" I asked.

"To make choices I suppose, right?" he responded.

"Precisely. And this happens without God's influence. You reap what you harvest. This is the only way we can be held accountable on the Day of Judgement."

"True, but may I interject?"

"Sure!"

"The Quran also contains other verses that clearly indicate a certain level of intervention from God that ultimately determine the outcome of our actions," he stated.

"Can you share some examples?" I asked.

"Well, to name a few, God says: 'You will not, except as God wills'[21] or 'God leaves to stray whom He wills and guides whom He wills'[22] or 'And whomsoever God wills to guide, He opens his chest wide with willingness towards self-surrender'[23] and a great many examples implying that God does determine the outcomes of some actions and intervenes to change things. If God doesn't actually get involved, and just observes, then why are we required to make requests of Him and make *dua*, or aspire to change a given state of affairs?"

"You are asking the right questions here for sure. You're headed in the right direction," I said with a smile.

"As long as I go somewhere I'm okay!" he answered with a nervous chuckle.

"Here's the thing. If we realise that the verses of the Quran do imply two things that might seem contradictory, what are we, men and women of faith, to make of it? That the Quran is contradictory therefore we should put it behind us, or surrender to our understanding of *Ilm al-Ghayb* and insist that God included two seemingly contradictory notions in the Quran for a reason?"

"Definitely the latter!"

"Great. So what we're saying here is that some verses in the Quran assert human free will by default, and others imply that that free will is occasionally veered off by divine intervention. Is there anything illogical about that?"

"I guess not. It's just people in this day and age resent the idea that anything or anyone can restrict their free will."

"But our free will is restricted all the time!"

"How so?"

"We don't choose our parents, our birthplace, our race, our genetic predispositions etc."

"Sure. But all this happens before birth."

"Neither do we choose between breathing air or breathing underwater like fish, nor do we choose between flying like birds or burrowing the earth like gophers!"

"I didn't think about this before."

"We cannot control other people's choices. Someone might kidnap me and hold me hostage against my will. Someone else might randomly hit me with a car and ruin my weekend plans. Natural phenomena and disasters restrict our choices all the time. I have no control over all of that. Our free will is restricted all the time," I said.

"It's clear to me now."

"At the same time, and despite the inconveniences, we still do have free will to make choices and decisions every day to the best of our abilities. When the alarm rings, we can either get up or snooze. I can either walk or drive to work. I can eat meat or vegetables. I can exercise or sit at home and watch TV. I can either pray or not. I can accept God as Lord or reject Him. I'm free to choose right?"

"Indeed."

"So what am I saying here?"

"That we both have free choice and lack free choice at the same time?" he answered with a question.

"Absolutely! And this is why the Quran bears both meanings. There are matters in which there is no choice and there are matters in which there is."

"So when does God interfere and when does He not?"

"Aha! For that, I need to define *qada* and *qadr*!" I stated.

"Please do."

"Well, although they are often used synonymously in the tradition, in the sense that they both imply a degree of divine limitation to human free will, they are still different."

"How different?" he asked.

"Well, *qada*, as the word implies, means decree or judgement. It signifies finality and denotes God's irresistible presence and consummating laws. God's *qada* is equivalent to His master plan. These are the laws that don't change for anyone. Through them, God's will comes to pass, and because of them, human agency endures its greatest limitation."

"What's an example of *qada* then?"

"Well, the laws of physics, one's place of birth, one's genetic makeup, one's longevity etc." I answered.

"Fascinating! These are all factors that limit human free will but we never complain about them. What is *qadr* then?" he asked.

"Well, again as the word implies, *qadr* signifies divine fine-tuning of His creation and their journeys, destinies, and actions. Its root word *taqdeer,* which means means adjustment and apportioning. Through *qadr*, God interferes by inflicting trials and tribulations that will certainly create crossroads and generate choices. It's an extremely complex web of macroscopic and microscopic events and occurrences engendered by God to adjust and modify human activities. From a drop of rain, a falling leaf, or a beautiful deer crossing the meadows, to the smell of flowers, the sound of waterfalls, and the greenery of landscape. All factors that make us stop what we're doing and make choices. Keep going or observe? Listen to the waterfalls or the birds chirping? Take in the greenery of spring or wait for the snow's milk-white? When God endows you with the ability to sing, do you act upon it or not? Do you sing filthy profane songs or sublime sonatas that inspire and fill the hearts with the love of God? If you are born to a wealthy family, do you spend it on women and booze or mosques and orphans?

And so on."

"This is so deep…give me a second to take all this in," he said.

"Take your time!"

"So, *qada* obviously cannot change right?"

"Right."

"What about *qadr*?"

"Well, infection with a virulent microorganism might be your *qadr* in order for God to put you through the trial of illness, but perhaps there's a way to stop it from happening in the first place."

"What is that exactly?"

"Prayer!" I said with a smile.

"Oh yeah! Doesn't the Prophet Muhammad say that prayer and *qadr* wrestle each other in the heavens?"

"Precisely. So your prayers can and often do stop *qadr* from happening, or alter its course."

"This is very cool. But there's something missing in this narrative."

"What is it?"

"Well, if God already destined you through *qadr* to a certain course, illness, or whatever, then God determined your path with regard to that particular course, right?" he asked.

"Not necessarily. He put an obstacle in your path. You still have to be the one to choose one course or the other," I answered.

"But getting sick is a path in and of itself that only God can determine, right?"

"Correct, but even that can change with your prayer if God wills it."

"So which one was in God's decree in the first place?"

"All of them!"

"How?"

"See here, a logical observation of the world indicates that the trajectory of life we experience is but one possible occurrence of multiple possibilities that could have happened."

"Elaborate please?" he asked nervously.

"It means that for every happening in our lives, there are other happenings that could have occurred. And since they didn't occur in this particular trajectory, they could have occurred in other trajectories."

"So…there's another reality in which my nephew didn't lose his faith and I'm not talking to you?" he asked slowly with a bewildered voice.

"Theoretically," I answered with a smile.

"And how does this help us understand *qadr*?"

"In a significant way. Look here: in this existence of ours, where your nephew lost his faith, there were multiple ways for you to react. Ignore the matter, cut your nephew loose, talk to another Imam, lose your faith as well etc. You chose one possible trajectory, which is to do something about it and talk to me in particular. The way *qadr* works is that God determines a finite number of choices, or outcomes of your journey, trajectories if you will. They are all written, but you get to choose which one will actually come to pass!" I said.

"Can you give me an example?" he asked with confusion.

"Well, let's take the getting sick example. In one scenario, you were going to get infected by malaria, in the second scenario you were going to catch the flu, and in the third, you were going to get West Nile Virus (WNV). Because you chose not to travel to Africa for the planned safari, you ended up not catching malaria or WNV, but just caught the flu because you didn't take your precautions when you hugged your cousin who was sick, and you could clearly see the symptoms. The three scenarios were all written, and you chose one."

"Oh Lord…so God essentially gives us multiple-choice questions?"

"Yes, with a finite list of possible outcomes!"

"Oh man!"

"I know. But hear me out. If God provides us with a finite number of choices, because this world is finite, but still gives us the power to pick one of them on our own, then for each of our actions, who is responsible?"

"Both us and God?"

"Thank you. I rest my case," I said with a smile.

"But wait! You said that God gave us multiple choices, I get that, but if I chose one or the other, then God must have known that I was going to make that choice in the first place and would have written it down?"

"You are still subjecting God to time I see. Do I need to go back to our discussion on time?"

"Oh no - sorry. I see your point now. There's no such thing as God knowing our 'future' choices since He's not limited by time. He sees all of our lives at once."

"Exactly," I said with a smile of relief.

"But I know this question will come up. This is really great reasoning. Can it be supported through tradition? Quran, *hadith* etc?

"I thought you'd never ask!"

He responded with an amused chuckle.

"Let's take a look at what God said in the scripture. Take for instance God annuls or confirms whatever He wills, for with Him is the mother of the book.'[24].This implies that God eliminates or affirms from the possible choices whatever He wills, based on human agency, but ultimately He has knowledge of all things, since He possesses the mother of books, or the source of all knowledge. This is why some companions of the Prophet Muhammad used to pray using similar language. Ibn Masud for instance used to say: 'Lord, if you had already decreed that I will be among the joyous, then confirm my destiny as such, for you eliminate or affirm as you wish!'[25] It is also reported that Umar Ibn Al-Khattab used to say: 'Lord, if you had already decreed that I will be among the miserable, then eliminate that and affirm me among the joyous!'[26]"

"Interesting. What else would the tradition say in support of this?" he asked.

"If God's decree is confirmed and inevitable, then there would be no room to ask God to change it right?"

"Definitely!"

"Well, in the famous *dua al-qunut* prayer, what do we say? 'Divert from us the worst of what You have decreed!'[27]."

"Oh yeah! I never thought of that."

"What do you think it implies?"

"That there are multiple possibilities and we pray for God to move us from one to the other!" he answered.

"Glad you figured this one out!"

"What else?"

"In another famous tradition, God says in *hadith qudsi*: 'I will always meet my worshipper's best expectations of me.'[28] Do you remember this one?"

"Yes. Always a beautiful prayer to bring comfort to the heart."

"What do you make of it?"

"Not sure - what?"

"That God can only meet our best expectations of Him, if and only if there are multiple ways to think of our destiny, and multiple ways to have expectations of God, and from those multiple ways, we pick the one that is most fitting to God's grace and majesty and assume this is the course that God will choose for us, and this is God's will that comes to pass. I can say God will either make my life miserable, average or amazing, so I pick amazing and put my effort in it and pray on it. This implies that there were possible scenarios and God chose one based on our expectations of Him," I said.

"This is incredibly cool!"

"Another one. God says in the Quran: 'And whatever strikes you of disaster - it is the result of what your hands have earned.'[29]" What do you think of this one?"

"That we should take responsibility for our own choices and own up."

"Which implies that God is...what?" I asked.

"That God is not the one that made us do it?"

"Exactly. Which also implies that our destiny is in our hands and is born of our choices. And although the choices are finite, at the end of the day it is us that have to make a choice and pull the trigger. When we commit sins, what is it that God expects us to do?"

"Return to Him and repent of course."

"Well, if your destiny is set, and the sinner is inevitably going to hell, then what's the point of repentance, unless with our human decisions we moved on to a different trajectory of what God made available to us?"

"I see. What about the famous *hadith* that says that in our mother's womb an angel comes to us and will dictate our *rizq* or provision, our *ajal* or longevity, deeds, and whether we're happy or miserable? Is the *hadith* weak or questionable?"[30]

"Aha! This is a really important *hadith* with a strong chain, and it was mentioned in both Bukhari and Muslim, so it cannot be easily escaped by attributing weakness to its *isnad* chain. On the other hand, it was used repeatedly to justify the fatalistic mentality of many Muslims, perpetuating the 'it's all written, so what's the point' kind of attitude."

"I know! I heard it being used many times in this context."

"True. And that's why we need to discuss it. First, it addresses *rizq* and *ajal*, which I plan to talk about in a minute. But let's focus on deeds and whether someone is happy or unhappy. The *hadith* at face value implies that your destiny is 'dictated' at birth and it becomes inescapable, right?"

"Yes!"

"And why do we reach this conclusion, from the language of the *hadith*?"

"Well, because it explicitly says that the angel will come and dictate your destiny," he said.

"And what's the word that is used here that implies this understanding?"

"The word write or dictate."[31]

"Could there possibly be another meaning to the word, or another contextual usage?" I asked.

"Well, the word 'write' is used occasionally to denote document, or record."

"Well, what if the job of that angel is NOT to dictate, but rather record that person's destiny as it is manifested in God's knowledge?"

"But then none of it has happened yet? How would the angel know what to write?"

I looked at him with agitated piercing eyes.

"Oh no - I did it again, didn't I? Okay. I see what you're saying. Since time is not a factor for God, He already knows our choices, and He commands the angel to just record those choices once we are born," he said apologetically.

"Exactly. Sort of like attaching your life's manifesto to your journey. This doesn't imply any interference from God in the choices involved in that journey, except for the matters of *qadr*, and providing you with a list of finite choices that I elaborated on earlier."

"Man...the more I learn I realise how ignorant I am!" he said.

"Imam Shafi'i used to say the same thing," I said amusingly. "It's a sign of humility."

"I hope so. But wait, you said you wanted to talk about *rizq* and *ajal*?"

"Yes! Because most people think that the amount of material acquisition they make in this world, also known as *rizq*, or the amount of time they will spend in this world, known as *ajal*, are both fixed by God's destiny."

"Are they not?"

"Not exactly."

"Oh God. Another lifelong assumption of mine is about to get shattered," he said with discomfort.

"Hear me out. On what basis are we saying that *rizq* is predetermined?"

"On the basis of many Quranic verses, prophetic traditions and the consensus of the scholars!"

"Can you share some examples?" I asked him.

"Well, take for instance the verse in the Quran: 'It is We who distribute their means of livelihood among them in the life of this world.'[32] Or: 'And there is no living creature on earth but depends for its sustenance on God,'[33] indicating clearly that your *rizq* is determined by God and can only come from Him, and that no amount of human effort can increase it and no amount of human negligence can decrease it!" he stated.

"Very interesting. I may disagree with your deductions, but I'll entertain the argument. Can you think of other citations?"

"I can also think of the *hadith* in which the Prophet said: 'Jebril revealed to me that no soul will die until it fulfils its *rizq*.'"

"Yes. This is a *hadith* that was mentioned in the Musnad of Imam Ahmad[34]."

"So...?"

"You make me laugh sometimes," I said with a big smile.

"Why?" he asked grudgingly.

"Because you are really sincere about learning but still give in to platitudes and commonly accepted knowledge that makes no sense!"

"I'm here aren't I?"

"That you are. And that's why I smile."

"So, what do we do about *rizq*?" he asked impatiently.

"First of all, none of what you mentioned states that there's a restriction on our ability as humans to earn more and have more. Just a ceiling that cannot be breached."

"In layman's terms, please!"

"What I mean is that God may set a limit to what you can earn in the life of this world. He can assign a share for you that no one will ever have. But at the end of the day, it is only through your human effort that this share will be obtained. If you don't flip every rock and knock on every door, you may very well live and die without having your full share. And most people don't."

"But the *hadith* says no one will die before they have acquired their *rizq*?"

"No, that's not what it says. It states that every soul will not die until it has complete access to its *rizq*. You still have to put in the effort to acquire it," I said firmly.

"So my *rizq* is not going to follow me everywhere and sit at my doorstep as my grandmother used to say?" he asked.

"Some of it will, but I'm afraid the vast majority of it is sitting out there somewhere waiting for you to hustle for it!"

"Oh man! So what's the point of assigning *rizq* if it's not guaranteed?"

"In order to quell men's anxiety and help them feel that they don't have to compete with one another, and take from each other what is not rightly theirs. The only obstacle between you and your share of the material world is not the possibility of someone else taking it, rather, it's your effort and ingenuity. We're not in competition with anyone to acquire our *rizq*. Our greatest competitor is our laziness!" I said.

"This is really eye-opening."

"Second, if *rizq* is assigned and will come to us no matter what, then it would logically follow that there is no way for it to increase as a result of human effort, or decrease it because of our negligence or sins, right?"

"I suppose so."

"Yet, the tradition suggests otherwise. In the very famous *hadith*, the Prophet Muhammad says: 'If you are God-conscious the way you should be, He would provide for you the way He provides for birds: They leave their nests hungry and return full'.[35] What does the *hadith* suggest?"

"That God will provide more for us if our consciousness of Him increases?"

"Definitely. Which also implies what?"

"That God-consciousness increases *rizq*?"

"Yes! But let me share more *hadiths* on this subject. The Prophet also says: 'A worshipper will be denied *rizq* as a result of a sin he/she committed.'[36] What does this imply?"

"That our *rizq* can actually decrease as a result of our sins!"

"Thank you."

"Okay. I totally concede here. But I think that when it comes to *ajal*, the matter is a lot clearer. One's longevity, and how long one will stay on this earth is absolutely determined by God and has nothing to do with human action or choice," he stated.

"How so?"

"Because there's a plethora of evidence on it. And please don't tell me my entire life was a lie on this one as well!"

"What is that plethora of evidence?" I asked gently.

"Well, God says: 'For when the term given by God is accomplished, it cannot be put forward,'[37] and 'When their term is reached, not an hour can they cause delay, not an hour can they advance.'"[38]

"Okay. Sounds pretty strong I have to agree."

"Right?"

"No. Wrong."

"How? Why?"

"Well, the two verses you cited were revealed in the context of nations and not individuals. The *ajal* that God was referring to references reaching the term of a particular nation, and not that of individuals. One of them is about the people of Noah, and the other one is more generic, in which God says in the preceding statement: 'there is a term limit for each nation.'"[39]

"What about the verse where God says: 'But to no soul will God grant respite when the time appointed for it has come.'"[40] This one clearly talks about an individual soul and not a nation?" he asked.

"Was hoping you'd bring this one up."

"And?"

"Well, before I address this, I want to cite some verses and *hadiths* that may bear a different meaning. Take the following for example: 'None that is long-lived has his days lengthened, nor is a part lessened from his days, but is in a decree ordained.'"[41]

"Wait! This implies that one's age can actually get longer or shorter! I never thought of it this way before!"

"I'm not done yet. In this particular verse, God lays it out clearly: 'It is He who created you from the earth, and then decreed a stated term for you. And there is in His presence another determined term!'[42] What does this one tell you?" I asked him.

"That there are two types of *ajal*!" he answered.

"Indeed."

"What? How come?? This goes against everything I grew up learning!"

"What you grew up learning is not a reference of knowledge, no offence."

"None taken, but please tell me more!"

"You might want to sit down because the *hadiths* will push you to the limit even further!"

"I am sitting down!"

"It is a figure of speech. I meant brace yourself!" I said with a suppressed laugh.

"Please stop torturing me."

"Okay! In the *hadith*, the Prophet is reported to have said: 'The only thing that stops *qadr* is *dua* and the only thing that increases one's life is acts of kindness!'[43] I already addressed the *qadr* discussion earlier."

"This is incredible!"

"I know. Here's another one: 'Whomsoever would be pleased to have more *rizq* and to live a longer life, let him/her maintain his/her kin.'[44] Here the Prophet ﷺ clearly says that keeping good ties of kinship gives you a longer life! Or the *hadith* in which the Prophet says: 'maintaining kinship, good manners and being a good neighbour bring blessings to one's dwelling and prolongs life.'"[45]

"Yeah!"

"In fact, Imam Shawkani has a book dedicated entirely to this subject, in which he argues that there are so many human actions that will contribute to living longer or shorter,"[46] I said.

"So one's *ajal* is not written at the time of their birth?"

"Of course it is."

"Wait, what? Didn't you just cite a whole bunch of sources suggesting otherwise?"

"The key to resolving any seeming contradiction in the discourse within the tradition on longevity and whether our age is assigned or not lies in drawing a line between two terms that were wrongfully used synonymously," I stated.

"What are those two words?"

"*Ajal* and *umr*."[47]

"So *ajal* is the one we've been seeing in the *hadiths*. What about *'umr*?" he asked.

"*ajal* implies an assigned end. The extent of how long one will live. The word bears determination and a divine decree. *'Umr* on the other hand implies the number of years one will live, without the same determination that *ajal* implies."

"So what are we saying here?"

"That *ajal* defines the absolute extent of one's life on this earth; your expiration date if you will. Your actions in this life will determine whether you will live that long or not. So *ajal* is equal to or greater than *'umr*. All verses or *hadiths* that imply divine determination use the word *ajal*, while the ones implying human action as a factor use *'umr*".

"So *'umr* can be lengthened but *ajal* not?"

"Precisely. So it is possible that someone's *ajal* was going to be 90 years, but because of their poor health choices they only lived to be 60," I said.

"This would definitely resolve the intellectual conflict between divine assignment of life and suicide," he said.

"For sure."

"What about murder? Or dying in a car accident caused by a drunk driver?"

"That would be *qada*, reflected in your *ajal*. It's definitely assigned by God. You just reached your expiration date."

"So with acts of kindness, honouring one's parents, or maintaining the ties of kinship, one's *'umr* will increase, but will end before or once it hits the *ajal*, right?"

"Glad you finally absorbed this."

"It's an amazing feeling!"

"In modern times, science has proven beyond doubt that people who live with families and strong support systems or married with children, usually live longer and healthier lives. Do you want to know my theory to explain this?" I asked.

"What?"

"I think it's because you have many loving people around you to pray for you all the time, which will eventually change your fate, or *qadr*, with God's leave!"

"This is quite the hypothesis!"

"As I said, our perception of divine decree versus human agency needs to be balanced. Our journey in this life is determined by both. And this is a very comforting thought."

"Without a doubt. But I have a question: why does God need to determine our lives in any measure? Why not just let us make our choices and be held accountable? I mean I understand that our lives are an outcome of both divine intervention and human free will. Why not just make it about human free will alone?" he asked.

"This would be very consequential. First, it would completely undermine the value of prayer. What's the point of talking to God at all if everything is incumbent upon human agency? Imagine living in a world where God simply doesn't help because any help would be considered a suspension of human free will, therefore rejected."

"That would be bleak," he said.

"For sure. Second, maintaining this balanced view of existence is healthy for your faith. If you believe in God, you must accept Him as an arbiter. As someone who knows better than you and wants what's best for you and one that is interested in your success and wants you to make it to heaven. It involves a good amount of strong faith to surrender your affairs to God; to accept His decree; to be content with His choices, even if you cannot see the immediate wisdom behind them. To think of God as your commanding officer and of yourself as a soldier. You still fight and pull the trigger, but you have to trust your officer when He commands you to advance here or there. After all, He's the one that sees the map and fathoms the bigger picture of the war. You are just one soldier in a battle," I said.

"This is very powerful."

"Thank you."

"Now with this out of the way, allow me to ask the cliché question that seems to bother everyone, which appears to be the last remaining issue for me, I think."

"What could that be?" I asked.

"The question of evil. Many people in this day and age lose their faith because of all the war and carnage that are rampant in the world when bad things happen to good people who are God-loving and try to do the right thing. People ask questions like: if God is so loving, why does He allow evil to thrive in the world? Why does He allow children to suffer and die? Why does He allow terrible things to happen to good people? Why does He let bad people get away with their egregious acts?"

"I see."

"I personally know people who completely lost their faith because of the dilemma of evil."

"Very sad. But let me ask you a question: what have we been talking about this whole time?" I asked.

"Well, God's choice versus human choice, right?" he answered.

"Exactly. And what is it that people are struggling with when it comes to choice?"

"Trying to make sense of a reality where God makes choices on our behalf, yet we are held accountable for them."

"And with the question of evil in the world, what is it that people expect God to do?"

"To use His might and power to stop evil of course," he answered.

"And what does God need to do in order to stop evil people from committing evil acts?"

"I don't know. Make them?"

"And in order to make them, what does God need to do to their free will?"

"Uhm...suspend it I guess, right?"

"Precisely! So here's the irony. Humanity rejects a reality in which God makes decisions for them and pauses their free will, yet demands a reality in which He does exactly that! We are just selective and want to tell God when to suspend our free will and when to let it run amok. Does this make sense to you?" I asked.

"I see your point. So evil happens in the world because free will is important to God?"

"Without any doubt. We need to make up our minds. If we want a world in which we are responsible and accountable and do things out of our free will, then we have to accept the very important consequence of freedom, and that is people will choose to do bad things with it sometimes."

"But most people still agree that a loving God should not allow for evil to exist in the first place. How do we respond to that?"

"By asking them this: are we arguing that evil and God are mutually exclusive, or are we trying to understand the wisdom behind God allowing evil to exist? Because there is no logical foundation to assume that God and evil cannot coexist," I said.

"Most would just ask how could an omniscient, omnipotent and omnipresent God allow for terrible things to happen to honest and loving people?" he said.

"The reason people think like this is because their minds have been rewired as a result of their postmodern experience."

"What does that mean?"

"It's ironic that people who live in poor countries, or people who lived in pre-modern times, would actually get closer to God in the aftermath of evil. Only in wealthy countries, and a post-modern world that evil acts push us away from God, not closer."

"What do you attribute this to?"

"Our perceptions of pleasure and pain."

"How so?"

"We live in a world where everyone thinks that the ultimate objective of this life is to pursue some type of an elusive state of happiness, and anything that interrupts that is considered bad. This usually happens to people who consider this life to be the end of all existence, and therefore any interruption of the constant pursuit of pleasure in this life becomes evil. Men and women of faith, on the other hand, think differently of the life of this world. For us, this entire journey is but a small phase in our existence, and after death, our souls will travel to another domain and will live on. Challenges, pain, suffering, and other forms of interruption are part of the journey. They prepare us for what comes next. They create stepping stones for us to ascend. The immovable boulder of evil is a building block that helps us rise spiritually," I said.

"But how does evil serve the purpose of helping us rise?"

"When we realise that every ounce of success in this life takes place after a period of struggle. Parents deprive their children of certain pleasures for their own good. Experiencing pain at the gym to stay healthy. Staying up all night for weeks studying for an upcoming exam. Forest fires make the soil very fertile. Revolutions and war bring peace and democracy. And the examples are innumerable. Why can't we assume the same about God, that He allows evil actions to be carried out as part of human free will because this is how humanity as a whole learns and grows, and this is how good becomes well defined and precious, and this is how heaven and hell, and the test of life, become meaningful?"

"I'm not disagreeing with you. But some will respond and say God is All-Powerful. He doesn't need this complex test of evil in order to gauge the veracity of our claims or to make us deserving of His grace. Why not just let us live happy lives free of evil?" he asked.

"Let me ask you a question first: who's responsible for evil acts?"

"Usually other human beings, I suppose."

"So who causes evil?"

"Man?"

"Why blame God for it then? Why shouldn't we as a human society hold each other accountable, and admit responsibility for the existence of evil, and do what we can, using our free will, to minimise its impact?"

"But evil is not just a product of human action. Sometimes seemingly evil outcomes are attributed to acts of nature, the source of which is ultimately God Himself?"

"Are you talking about forest fires, mudslides, hurricanes etc, and other disasters that are caused by man's tampering with nature, pollution, man-made climate shift, and the likes of these events?" I said sarcastically.

"Well, no. I'm talking about earthquakes, volcanic eruptions, and other such events that have nothing to do with man's egregious activities."

"Okay. Fair enough. What bothers us so much about those catastrophic events?"

"The sheer death and destruction of course!" he answered.

"Okay. Let's take for example one earthquake, and say about 100,000 died in its aftermath. This would be tragic, right?"

"Of course!"

"What if I told you that according to the UN, about 100 people die every minute?"

"That's terrible!"

"Which means that there are over 6,000 deaths per hour, or about 150,000 deaths per day, on any given day!" I said.

"This is absolutely horrifying!"

"It is, but I don't see you getting upset about it every day."

"What do you want me to say?"

"That the reason we get upset at natural disasters, and start hurling accusations against God, is because of the sheer death that takes place during open events and gets highlighted by the media and gets ingrained in our memory. Death does happen every day as part of the natural process of life and it shouldn't offend us when it happens in large numbers as a result of a natural disaster, and if it did, it shouldn't blind our judgement to accuse the Creator of what He didn't commit."

"Okay...this is cruel but honest. Still, why does God allow for this sheer death to take place when He can easily stop it?"

"At what cost will He? Natural disasters at the end of the day are a byproduct of the natural process of the world and following to the letter its physical laws. In order for God to stop this from happening, He would have to suspend those laws and make miracles or tamper with the parameters of the system He put in place. To what end will He do this?"

"Because it's too painful."

"Well, men and women of faith believe that life is. This world is not the end of all things. Death is a bridge to another domain, another existence, and another life. Pain is part of that experience and an integral part to it," I stated.

"I think I'm satisfied. This was really illuminating! I'm sorry it took this long. Thank you!"

"No worries. You're welcome. By the way, does your nephew still have the *hikmah* keychain?"

"I check in a subtle way every time I meet him, and yes, he carries it! Don't know what that means."

"*Alhamdulillah*," I said with gratitude.

"See you next time!" he said.

"Sure. Take care."

*Chapter 9*

# LGBTQA+

It was a delightful Sunday morning. The spring breeze blew calmly through the trees. Sun rays made their way through the branches and cast a beautiful interrupted shade onto the soccer field. It was the perfect morning for a game. I ran through the field, trying to fight my exhaustion, as I competed with 15-year-olds. Between the sounds of laughter, the goalie's instructions to the team, and the occasional cheer by the small audience on the bleachers, it felt that all the excitement in the world was teleported to our mosque's lush green soccer field. As the game went on, I accidentally gazed into the bleachers looking for my wife. And there he was, sitting at the edge of the bleacher, restlessly, and once I made eye contact with him, he gave me a nervous gesture of greeting. I could see the urgency in his face, and I knew that it was going to be another two hour conversation with the agonised uncle. I respectfully asked the referee for an exchange, greeted my fellow players with a big smile, and walked out to grab a towel, after which I was planning to head straight to him.

"Imam, can you believe that the City of New York recognises 31 different gender identities?" These were the words I heard as my sweaty forehead was still buried in the towel. I turned around, and there he was, standing nervously less than two feet away. His voice was filled with more consternation than usual.

"Oh hey! Assalamualaikum!" I said.

"Wa alaykum assalam! Sorry, the thoughts in my head are racing," he said apologetically.

"No worries. It's a beautiful morning. Let's walk to that bench and talk."

We made our way to a picnic table in a shaded area next to the field and sat down.

"So you were talking about the City of New York's gender recognition," I said, prodding him to continue.

"Yes! More than 31 genders, I tell you. Have you heard of this before?" he asked urgently. "Actually I didn't know it was that many!" I responded with shock and a controlled tone of humour, followed by a nervous chuckle.

"Some of the genders on the list are gender-bender and gender-blender!"

"Yep," I responded with a big smile.

"It's not funny!" he retorted while shaking his head in disbelief.

"I wasn't laughing at the challenge. Just at your response," with a smile on my face, trying to make light of the huge cultural shock he was experiencing.

"My nephew told me last week that his childhood best friend came out as a transgender person, and that he plans to support him!"

"I see…and how did you respond?" I asked.

"I told him this is not the way God wanted us to live."

"What did he say?"

"He said if God does exist, then He's the one that created people the way they are. Gay, trans, bisexual, whatever. It's either their genetics or God. Either way, it's not their choice and we have to support them."

"It's clear to me that your nephew is coming to you with all these questions because the gears in his head are grinding at full speed. He shares this with you begging for a response that would quell his intellectual restlessness."

"I can see that. But to be completely honest with you, I myself am a bit confused," he said with frustration.

"Why do you say that?"

"I don't know. On the one hand, Islam prohibits homosexuality and changing one's gender -I think- so we cannot condone the whole LGBTQ thing, but on the other hand, it's his childhood friend! What am I supposed to say?"

"Well, you're mixing many things up. You mentioned homosexuality, LGBTQ, changing gender, and Islamic prohibition in the same breath."

"So what?"

"Let's unpack this whole thing and address it one piece at a time because it's not all the same."

"Okay." he responded with ambivalence.

"First, let's talk about homosexuality," I said.

"Sure, but the transgender thing is connected because ultimately once one changes their gender, they will assume a different gender identity and may develop sexual desires or engage in sexual behaviour with what should be considered the same gender, right?"

"You're mixing things up again," I said firmly.

"Okay, sorry. Please go ahead," he answered apologetically.

"You're calm?"

"Yes. I swear," with a nervous smile on his face.

"Okay. Here goes. First, we can talk about homosexuality and then unpack the whole LGBTQ thing. Agreed?"

"Sure."

"There are multiple things involved with the word "homosexuality". First, there's same-sex attraction. Second, there is same-sex activity. Third, there is same-sex marriage as an individual choice. And finally, there's same-sex marriage as a social discourse and whether Muslims should condemn it or support it," I said.

"Wow!"

"And after you have tackled homosexuality with its multifaceted questions, you will then have enough intellectual capital to address the remainder of the LGBTQA+ ethos, including gender transformation."

"Now I'm excited!" he said, with clear signs that his confusion and anger were starting to be replaced with pure curiosity.

"Great. So first, we need to establish that thinking about prohibited acts and committing them are two different things. The Prophet Muhammad ﷺ was very clear about this in the *hadith*: 'God has pardoned this nation for the thoughts and obsessions of the mind, as long as no words are uttered or actions have been taken.'"[48]

"What does that mean?" he asked.

"It means that God does not hold us accountable for the thoughts that cross our minds, even if they are wrong or inappropriate. Only the actions we take or the words we say that will matter when we stand before the Creator on the Day of Judgement," I answered.

"Are you saying that having lustful thoughts about someone, for example, would be okay?" "I didn't say that it would be okay. I said that it merely doesn't count as a sin, because it's not easily controlled. Ultimately, the more we obsess about something, the stronger the likelihood we'd eventually act upon it. So we should always try to avoid spending too much time thinking about and fantasising over things that the Creator has prohibited, and we should always seek refuge in God from those thoughts."

"I guess that makes sense. But how is this related to homosexuality?" he asked curiously.

"Well, the word homosexual might mean someone who just has tendencies, or desires, who might 'think' about homosexual relations or possess the attraction to the same gender, without necessarily engaging in sexual acts. Would that in and of itself be prohibited?"

"I suppose not."

"Great. The challenge is that most people in this age assume that they somehow need to 'act' upon any desires they might possess. As a man of faith you might have same-sex desires, but religious law and most scholars are not interested in thoughts or desires. Their concern was and always has been with actions. Many folks think that these debates are postmodern and progressive, while classical scholars have addressed them over a millennium ago. Just like their Greek counterparts, many notables in Islamic history marvelled over the beauty of young beardless boys, called *Amrad,*[49] and wrote poetry about them, prompting scholars to recommend that men should lower their gaze upon seeing those good looking beardless boys. This fascination with boys was considered awkward, but certainly not prohibited unless it led to illicit activities," I stated.

"But homosexuality is not a choice. It's all genetically determined right? How can we ask those who have the desire not to act upon it? If one has this overwhelming disposition that is part of their nature, wouldn't it be unfair to tell them not to act upon it and live a lifetime of longing and deprivation?"

"You're making assumptions and mixing things up again," I said.

"How?"

"There's no conclusive scientific study or biological evidence yet that homosexuality is genetically determined. It's all conjecture at this point. So we cannot say that homosexual behaviour or same-sex desires are borne out of nature."

"I didn't know that."

"I will assume though, for the sake of argument, that homosexual desires are genetically determined. Even then, I would say that the existence of desire doesn't in and of itself permit action in the sight of God. You're a heterosexual male, for example. If this is genetically determined, does it give you a proper excuse to act promiscuously with women?"

"Of course not, but a simple response to this is that heterosexuals have a 'natural' outlet to satisfy their desires, while homosexuals don't. Since one can either be homosexual or heterosexual and if we agree that gay marriage is religiously prohibited, how is it fair then to allow heterosexuals to marry while disallowing homosexuals?" he asked.

"This assumption is also false. Sexuality according to the vast majority of scientists is a continuum. The binary perception of sexual orientation -that humans are strictly predisposed to be either heterosexual or homosexual or bisexual- is not the accepted scientific and philosophical position among most researchers anymore. In fact, Alfred Kinsey, Fred Klein, and other sexuality scholars stated unequivocally that sexuality is a dynamic, multivariable process that is influenced by culture, behaviour, fantasies, social preferences, and emotions."

"This is intriguing!"

"Moreover, the official position of the American Psychological Association is that sexual orientation exists along a continuum that ranges from exclusive heterosexuality to exclusive homosexuality and includes various forms of bisexuality."

"I see. But my question here is: would that orientation change by human choice?"

"I say it does, all the time. Sexual orientation is fluid. Professed homosexuals may engage in heterosexual relations and vice versa. Now for politically correct purposes, scholars and scientists in the West distinguish between sexual orientation, which is presumably unchangeable, and sexual identity, which is changeable. But ultimately, we see self-professed homosexuals who have an attraction to the opposite gender and heterosexuals who might occasionally engage in homosexual activities. This is the reality," I said.

"The plot thickens..."

"It does, but that's not our concern. What we men and women of faith worry about is God's pleasure. What I'm trying to get at in this conversation is that having same-sex desires while certainly not deterministic, is not necessarily prohibited by the letter of Islamic law either, unless that translates to actual sexual contact with the same gender."

"But this doesn't answer the question of marriage and intimacy. If people with heterosexual desires can still marry in a religiously acceptable way, how is it fair to demand of people with homosexual tendencies to never get married, and to never experience intimacy, since homosexual marriages are religiously prohibited?" he asked sincerely.

"Let me respond with a question: is sexual intimacy required for survival?"

"I suppose not. Although we all desire it, we can certainly live without it."

"Great. So if the Creator chose not to grant someone the ability to experience something that is not required for survival, why do we think that it's unfair?"

"Well, it may not be required for survival, but sexual experience with a partner is certainly one of the pleasures of this world, and losing it, or missing out on the opportunity to experience it in a way that pleases God, is definitely frustrating, isn't it?"

"Frustrating, but not devastating. God in His wisdom deprives us of things all the time. How many people come to this world with congenital anomalies? How many men are quadriplegic and will be in a wheelchair their entire lives and will never experience sex? If I told you that you can come to this world with two choices: either you have a heart problem and will die at the age of 25, or come to the world without the ability to have sex but will live long and healthy, which one would you choose?" I asked.

"Well, personally I'd opt for option two, but I know many men who would go with option one," he said with a loud laugh.

"I agree. But my point is that the inability to experience sex should not be a deal-breaker in terms of our relationship with God. I don't have to act upon whatever I feel without scrutiny and without consideration. Homosexuality, while real, must be thought of as a test from God, and one must do what they can to keep their faith intact and endeavour to pass the test. Will we fall into error and sin occasionally? Sure. We're only human. But normalising sin and sinful lifestyle in the name of biological tendencies rips man of agency and free will," I said decisively.

"This is a powerful point. I think I'm satisfied. Moving along to the second point that we discussed earlier: same-sex activities. What's the religious evidence that prohibits this behaviour?"

"It is unfortunate that we live in an age when we really have to get into the nitty-gritty of whether engaging in homosexual acts is religiously prohibited or not."

"Don't mean to cross any lines. Forgive me. Just trying to wrap my head around this whole thing once and for all and be ready with all answers," he said.

"To the contrary. I'm glad we're having this conversation."

"Great!"

"Are homosexual acts, meaning engaging in sexual relations of any sort with the same gender, permissible or prohibited in Islam? The answer is prohibited of course, without a single shred of doubt. Aside from the so-called progressive Muslim movement, which is a small fringe group of Western Muslim liberal intellectuals, we're not aware of a single credible voice that has granted sanction to homosexual behaviour. The Quran is clear in condemning the acts of the People of Prophet Lot, who lived in the City of Sodom when God says to its men: "And remember Lot when he said unto his people: will you commit abominations such as none in all the world has ever done before you? Verily you approach men with lust instead of women, nay, but you are people that exceed all bounds!" after which God removes Lot and his family, saves his wife, and destroys the city.'"[50]

"May God protect us," he said with a sigh. "What about the *hadith*?" he asked.

"Good question. The Prophet Muhammad ﷺ says: 'God cursed anyone who commits the acts of the People of Lot!'[51] and he repeated this three times. Besides, it is also the consensus of the scholars across the ages that this is an abominable act that shakes the throne of the Lord," I said swiftly.

"I'm embarrassed to even say this, but I heard someone once say that the condemnation in the Quran of the People of Lot pertains to them practicing gang rape and not consensual homosexual behaviour, because the Quran speaks of the men putting Lot's house under siege wanting to rape his visitors, unbeknownst to them that they were angels that came to destroy them. How do you respond to this?" he asked.

"I'm aware of this argument, and it holds no water. First, if that's what God meant, He wouldn't have said to their men 'you lust for men and not women'.[52] Second, the incident of the men of Lot gathering around Lot's house to 'rape' what they assumed were good looking men that were visiting the city, is something that happened in the very last part of the story. Throughout his life as a Prophet, Lot had been admonishing his people and trying to get them to cease their abominable behaviour, which was not just rape, but consensual homosexual behaviour as well. Lot repeatedly tried to discourage men in his town from engaging in such acts by telling them: don't 'commit shameful deeds in your assemblies',"[53] I answered.

"I see."

"In addition to that, when the men came and surrounded Lot's house in order to abduct his male visitors and rape them, he offered their leaders to marry his daughters, not to have consensual homsexual relations with other men from the group! The Quran states this when God says: 'O my people! Take instead these daughters of mine, for they are purer for you!'[54]"

"But this brings up a question about gay marriage in particular. Perhaps the prohibition is not on homosexual relations per se. Isn't it possible that what God really meant was that any sexual behaviour outside of marriage is prohibited? After all, the Quran says: 'The true believers are supposed to preserve their private parts, meaning not have sex except with their wives or what their right hands possess.'[55] Can homosexual relations be legitimised through the union of marriage?" he asked.

"Do you think that God would make something abominable and then sanction it through marriage?" I asked sternly.

"Well, He does that with heterosexual marriage! Sex is prohibited but in a marriage it's permissible right?"

"You have a point there. Perhaps we might have to discuss this as well!"

"Sorry!"

"No worries. So, what is the definition of marriage in Islam?" I asked.

"Well, I'm not sure. A sacred union between man and woman?"

"Here's the mistake. Unlike the Christian tradition, there's nothing sacramental about marriage in Islam. It's not a holy union. It's not a sacred institution like we sometimes make it to be. It needs to be preserved and protected, but according to the letter of Islamic law, marriage is literally a contract."

"Hmm…a contract?"

"Yes. A contract. Marriage in Islam, stripped from all cultural addendums that Muslims have added to it over the centuries, is a contractual agreement between man and woman, stipulating that sexual relations, financial support and reproductive rights are exchanged between the married couple. I know this might impress our Western sensibilities in a different way, but this is just the letter of the law. There's a lot more to marriage than that obviously, but we need a definitive objective criterion to define what is and what is not marriage. Islam of course emphasises the value of love and partnership, and places significant importance on fidelity and loyalty, but ultimately, marriage is a legally binding agreement between a man and a woman where intercourse and reproductive rights are given in exchange for caring and financial support," I stated.

"Wow."

"I know. With this in mind, let me ask you: what is the only form of intercourse allowed in Islam?"

"The only form of intercourse that is permitted in Islam is vaginal. Right?" he said with shy hesitation.

"Correct. Anal intercourse is not permitted even between married heterosexual couples, right?"

"Yes."

"And if the only sanctioned form of intercourse is vaginal, then what does that tell you about the nature of marriage in Islam?" I asked.

"That it can only be a union between man and woman?"

"I rest my case," I said confidently.

"Wow - okay. But I have another question."

"Please!"

"If all forms of same-sex activities are prohibited in Islam, is there corporal punishment for the offence?"

"This is a loaded question!"

"I know, but it's really important because some people use *hudood* punishment as grounds to exact or justify violence against members of the LGBTQ community."

"Yes, and this is extremely unfortunate and totally unacceptable," I said.

"But you didn't answer my question. Is there a *hudood* punishment for homosexual behaviour?"

"Yes, there is," I said firmly.

"How is it unacceptable then?"

"Well, listen. Rousseau in *The Social Contract* argues that it is impossible to live in peace with those we regard as damned. I disagree with this. I live among neighbours who are not only non-Muslim, but many of them practice things that are in my judgement very harmful, such as promiscuous sexual behaviour, drinking alcohol, or engaging in gambling activities. In my opinion, if someone leads a life of vice such as that, they will be in trouble on the Day of Judgement, but does that prevent me from being a good neighbour to them? I still greet them in the morning, talk to them and even share sweets with them before Ramadan and Eid! Rejecting someone's lifestyle doesn't necessarily lead to violence against them!" I stated.

"I don't disagree with you on this. Nonetheless, it's still a cause for alarm for many that there is a physical punishment for same-sex activities in Islamic law. If God instituted corporal punishment for homosexual acts, what are we supposed to do and how can that be reconciled with your congenial perspective about those with whom we don't share the same moral paradigm?" he asked.

"I say this is a nonissue."

"How is it not? People use that as grounds for violence against homosexuals and members of the LGBTQ community!"

"People use religious arguments to propound all kinds of sinister behaviour, every day. The basic facts here are simple. While all schools of thought of Islamic law agreed that engaging in same-sex acts is prohibited, they differed with regard to the appropriate form of punishment for it. In the Hanafi perspective, the form of punishment is left to the judge and the ruler (*ta'zeer*). In the other three Sunni schools of thought, *liwat* (penetrative sex between males) is included with *hudood* punishments and is considered a death penalty offence. But there are two very important points to make here: first, the letter of Islamic law, as well as other ancient legal systems, was drafted at times when it was very difficult, if not nearly impossible for political authority to enforce the law. So creating laws that were very scary and severely harsh was necessary to achieve deterrence to discourage people from committing offences, as opposed to practically punishing them for those offences after they have been committed. This is why we seldom have reported cases where those corporal punishments were actually administered. Second, while it may have been true that a same-sex act was considered a death penalty offence by many scholars, the procedural safeguards of conviction that we see in cases of fornication, for example, were still applied, which made it nearly impossible for someone to be convicted of this offence if they knew the law and lived in a country in which such law is applied. Third, the application of those laws is a right reserved to rulers and judges, and not the masses. In other words, any violence perpetrated by the mob to exact violence on members of the LGBTQA community is immoral and antithetical to Islamic teachings and legal procedures, and is punishable under terrorism laws in *shariah*," I said.

"I'm satisfied with this response!"

"Good."

"But now that this has been resolved, let's move to the last point on the list. What about the legalisation of gay marriage? How are we as Muslims who live in Western societies supposed to grapple with this reality?"

"Ah. This is a very important conversation," I said.

"I mean we are already divided on this matter. Some Muslim groups have already come out in support of gay marriage on the grounds that it is a civil rights issue. Others support the right of gays to marry because we as Muslims are supposed to resist any popular definitions of marriage that are borne out of the Christian worldview since we Muslims may have marriage practices that are antithetical to that world view, such as polygamy etc. and we'd want our marriage practices to be recognised as well. Where are we supposed to stand?" he asked.

"I'm aware of the existence of a multitude of views in our community about gay marriage. I'm also aware of the fact that the gay community has been very supportive of our community in our civil rights plight in the West. I'm also aware that any possible rejection of gay marriage is often perceived as anti-gay or homophobic."

"So how should we walk this landmine then?" he asked.

"By being true to our tradition and our faith the best we can, discarding any political or social considerations," I stated unequivocally.

"What do you mean?"

"I mean being honest and sharing your religious positions with others in a cordial fashion, is better than acting in evasive ways, or subverting your own values to please one cultural phenomenon or the other. This is not healthy for our worldly purposes, and is certainly harmful from the point of view of the Hereafter."

"Can you elaborate?"

"First, after I have established to you how Islam perceives same-sex relations, how can we justify gay marriage by any stretch of the imagination? And if this is something that we consider to be harmful, how can we condone others when they practice it?"

"Are you saying that our pronounced position should be the rejection of gay marriage?"

"Without any equivocation!" I said.

"Wouldn't this hurt our relations with the gay community and portray Muslims as homophobic?"

"It shouldn't, if we clarify our position with compassion and empathy. The consumption of alcohol is forbidden in Islam. My neighbour drinks. I don't think he sees me as a hateful person who lacks compassion just because I don't condone drinking. Neither does he expect me to tell him drinking is perfectly okay. At the same time, I don't go out of my way preaching to people who drink that they need to stop. I acknowledge that I live in a diverse society and that people make choices that are not compatible with my moral system, and that's the reality, and it's okay. But at the end of the day, I have my values and I will stand up for them. And if given a chance, I would certainly pronounce those values and educate society about them. And if possible, I would even go as far as rallying society to adopt them using the available democratic means."

"So are you saying that you would support legislation that limits or prohibits the sale and consumption of alcohol?" he asked.

"If such a measure comes on a ballot I would."

"Wow. But wouldn't this be considered imposing our religion on others?"

"I don't think so. We're not voting to force people to convert to Islam or for women to cover. This is about making a public statement to curb the social effects of certain behaviour that is proven to be harmful and detrimental," I responded.

"But why not just keep our religious sentiment to ourselves?"

"Because if our religious sentiment is valid and beneficial in our eyes, why not at least share it with others and engage our society in a conversation that is inspired by it, without any violence or coercion? If Islamic teachings are so important and valuable to us, why are we burying them in the corridors of our mosques and the hallways of our homes, instead of using those teachings to bring relevance to our community and our faith, and utilise it as an instrument to resolve the chronic illnesses of the modern world? Why should we intentionally marginalise Islam?" I asked.

"I don't think that the intent is to marginalise Islam. Just keep it relevant between us Muslims and with those who are interested in its stance on matters and issues," he responded.

"This might certainly save us the social cost of speaking the truth, but is it healthy for us? If we don't stand up to keep the definitions of right and wrong alive and viable, then what do you think is going to happen?"

"Those definitions will keep evolving, I think..."

"They absolutely will, and they do already," I said.

"Agreed."

"Besides, if we as Muslims believe a certain act to be prohibited, how can we support legislation that sanctions it while still being true to our values and principles?"

"I don't think that's possible," he said.

"Precisely! God says: 'they who do not judge in accordance with what God has revealed are indeed unjust!'[56]"

"What about the argument that gay marriage is a civil rights issue that aims at bringing equity between citizens and eliminate discrimination against those who are not traditionally married?"

"This is resolved when the state gets its hands off marriage in general, and not expand its definition!"

"How so?"

"In my judgement, we are better off here adopting the libertarian view, that the state should not regulate any form of marriage, heterosexual or otherwise, and should then refrain from using marriage as a platform to grant citizens any privileges, tax benefits etc. This way traditionally married heterosexual couples will be on an equal playing field with others who choose different lifestyles. This is how you resolve the civil rights component and the tax disparity that the gay community complains about, and not by redefining the meaning of marriage," I said.

"But knowing that this is unlikely to be a reality anytime soon, wouldn't it be prudent to support any minority in their plight for recognition, and defend their rights, lest our Muslim community might also lose its rights to the same injustices? It would be a domino effect so to speak, no?" he asked.

"Well, first we need to agree that not recognising gay marriage is not a form of injustice in the first place. Second, marriage, any form of marriage, is a civil choice, not a civil right. Society doesn't have a responsibility to get people married, or recognise their marriages, opposite-sex or otherwise. And if this is the case, then choosing not to support what is not a right in the first place is not going to create a domino effect of compromising what is an essential civil right, such as religious freedom. Third, our Muslim community needs to be vigilant, that in the course of its refraining from supporting gay marriage, it needs to be at the forefront of supporting all people in our society, including homosexuals, to be treated equally before the law and for their choices, however much we might disagree with them, to be respected," I said.

"Fascinating! What about the argument that the Muslim community should support a more inclusive definition of marriage because Islamic marriage with its accepted polygamous practices and so on, would still be rejected in the West, therefore we're better off supporting gay marriage because it expands the definition of accepted marriage practices?"

"This is a very lame argument. First, how relevant is polygamy for Muslim communities in the West? Probably not that much. Second, if we go down this road, who's to say that we shouldn't support incestuous mariages, or other forms of deviance, in order to uphold one Islamic practice that is merely permissible? Third, since when do we use such utilitarian methods to establish what is *halal* and *haram*, or what is Islamically prescribed or prohibited?"

"You've made your point very clear!" he said with an amused chuckle.

"Thank you!"

"I did notice something though Imam. You keep saying LG-BTQA. I know what the first five letters stand for: lesbian, gay, bisexual, transgender, and queer. What does A stand for?"

"A stands for asexual."

"Asexual?" he asked with a sense of astonishment.

"Yes."

"What does that mean?"

"It references people who are not interested in sex the way the rest of us are. They may completely lack the desire, or perhaps they don't have enough motivation to make sex an important part of their lives."

"I feel very ignorant right now."

"Let me make matters worse. Do you know that some add another letter to the acronym? Some use LGBTQIA," I said.

"Lord! What does the "I" stand for?"

"It stands for Intersex!" I said ominously.

"What in God's name is that?"

"It describes people who may not necessarily fit in the genetic or biological characteristics of male and female. These variations may involve genital ambiguity such as having both male and female genital parts or chromosomal ambiguity other than the typical xx and xy phenotypes."

"I'm dizzy…"

"I can understand. Believe it or not, there are clearly stated Islamic positions that have been in our classical works for over a millennium about these orientations!" I said.

"Really?!"

"Yes. The Quran talks for instance about 'those with no sexual desire'[57] as exempt from the natural boundaries between men and women, so they can be in the presence of women who are not fully covered, and it won't be considered impermissible."

"This is incredible. Would this apply to Asexuals?"

"Possibly."

"Fascinating!"

"Moreover, there's Islamic guidance on the '*Khuntha Mushak-kal*'[58], or the mixed gender whose genital features are ambiguous, much like intersexuals," I said.

"This is amazing! And what did the scholars say about this?"

"Well, Ibn-Qudamah for instance says that if someone is inter-sex, they get married based on their own subjective presumption of their gender identity. If they feel they are more male than fe-male, they marry a female and vice versa! Imam Suyuti has sim-ilar views, but he argues that gender identification shouldn't be a matter of choice or subjective orientation, but physical and behav-ioural tendencies. If a person shows the predisposition of a female, they should act and behave and lead a life as a female for all Islamic purposes, including marrying a man if they so desire, and so on."

"Makes me feel proud of our legacy that the scholars addressed all this!" he said with a smile.

"Happy to hear this."

"But a question looms here, imam. What is the Islamic guid-ance on gender identity and transformation? Is it okay to adopt a different gender identity - different from the one you were born or raised with, or the one that reflects your genetic phenotype? Is gender determined by God or is it a social identity that can change or evolve?" he asked.

"Another loaded question!" I said.

"Sorry!"

"Well, let's break all this down. First, there is the question of effeminate behaviour by males or masculine behaviour by females that is born out of hormonal issues. And then there's the issue of '*tashabuh*'[59], where a male deliberately acts like a female, or vice versa, where the behaviour is engendered by the individual as a choice and not a product of hormonal determination. And then there's the question of gender dysphoria, where someone psychologically identifies with another gender that is not what they are born with, without a hormonal imbalance. And finally, there is the question of gender reassignment!"

"Oh God, you're doing it again!"

"What am I doing?" I said with a sarcastic smile.

"You're breaking down a big boulder into small little pieces to crush them one by one!" he said amusingly.

"Crush them or just address them," I said with a mischievous smile.

"I love it!"

"Okay. So let's get right to it. First, we need to establish that the gender that God created you with is a deterministic matter that is not subject to human whim or cultural consideration. It's a matter of *qada'*, or divine decree. You don't choose your gender any more than you choose your parents, your ethnic makeup, or your genetic predispositions. God says clearly in the Quran: 'To God alone does the dominion of heavens and earth belong. He creates whatever He wills. He bestows the gift of female offspring on whomever He wills, and the gift of male offspring on whoever He wills!'[60] Therefore, accepting God's decree and attempting not to change it, is part and parcel of being a believer," I said.

"That's a fair point."

"Second, effeminate behaviour by men, or masculine behaviour by women is not necessarily considered impermissible, as long as it is not being artificially manufactured for the sake of 'looking or acting like' the opposite gender. Ultimately, you're still expected to follow the religious considerations relevant to your gender of birth, for all practical purposes of Islamic law."

"I didn't know that."

"Third, as I mentioned earlier, there are those who cannot identify with either gender because of genetic or anatomical anomalies that make their gender identification difficult or ambiguous. In which case the scholars agreed that they still need to identify with one gender or the other, either subjectively or objectively."

"Yes, I got that part."

"Fourth, as I said earlier, *tashabuh* is not permissible. The idea of imitating the opposite gender for the fun of it, or trying to dress in clothes that are culturally known to be exclusive to the opposite gender, is not permissible. In the *hadith*, the Prophet Muhammad explicitly disparaged those who try to appear different than their gender of birth,"[61] I stated.

"But earlier you said a man acting effeminate or a woman acting masculine is okay?" he asked.

"As long as it happens unwittingly, and they are not trying to actively dress like the opposite sex and change their gender identity and behaviour."

"I see."

"Fifth, in some cases, someone is born genetically male or female, and due to hormonal imbalance and disorders, they are raised with another gender identity. Is it possible in this case to use corrective hormonal therapy to restore their birth sex? The answer is yes."

"This is really important! So you're saying that the only time it's okay to use hormonal therapy is when we are just restoring the original sex?"

"Yes, that's exactly what I'm saying. So this is not some elective hormonal therapy in order to alter one's gender at whim."

"Sounds good. However, some people may be genetically male or female, and they don't have any hormonal disorder, but they psychologically feel the desire to identify with another gender. Is there any Islamic guidance on this?" he asked.

"This condition is called Gender Dysphoria, where someone experiences the overwhelming feeling that one's emotional and psychological identity as male or female is opposite to one's biological sex. Of course, many folks today, particularly in the transgender community call for the complete declassification of this condition from the books of medicine and to stop assuming it's a medical condition in the first place. In this case, we would just accept someone's subjective gender preferences by granting them hormonal therapy or complete gender reassignment."

"Would this be Islamically acceptable?" he asked.

"Likely not. I've yet to find a credible scholar who has accepted the existence of gender dysphoria or allowed it to be used as grounds for altering one's gender identity. People who may have this condition may need psychotherapy or other forms of psychiatric help, which of course is becoming increasingly difficult in Western settings."

"I see. I guess the only remaining question is corrective surgery. What are the situations in which Islam allows for gender reassignment?"

"As I briefly mentioned before, invasive methods of gender reassignment, such as hormonal therapy and surgery, are only allowed in a 'restorative' sense, meaning bring to normal the state of someone's gender to become compatible with their biological sex, or making the phenotype compatible with the genotype, to use scientific terminology. For example, if someone is genetically male, but due to hormonal imbalance has exceptionally large breasts or other manifestations of recessive male traits, hormonal therapy can be administered and surgery can be used to "restore" that person's male identity. It is also permissible in the case of intersex individuals, where the only determining factor as to their gender is their subjective perception, in which case surgery is performed to achieve this restoration. Beyond this, there's not much room to maneuver. The only exception I saw to this rule was certain opinions held by modern Azhari scholars, such as Jad El-Haq and Tantawi, in which they argued that gender reassignment is permissible if a team of psychiatric experts agreed that surgery is the only way to treat someone's gender dysphoria, even if the new gender is not compatible with their biological sex," I said.

"I'm just fascinated that such conversations were had by the scholars and how diverse their views were!"

"The views are diverse, but the majority opinion is strong and very clear."

"Can I ask one last question? I promise!"

"By all means!"

"Many young Muslims in the West struggle to understand and grapple with the transgender question. They grow up with kids that one day 'come out' and decide to change their gender, or identify with no gender. How are they supposed to treat them? Based on their original or acquired gender identity? Can they still be friends with them? How would marriage, *mahram*[62], and *awra*[63] considerations work?" he asked.

"It's interesting you ask this question. A few weeks ago a young sister in our community came to me with a similar dilemma. She said that her childhood friend, a female, came out as a boy and decided to pronounce a different gender identity. Her question was this: should I just treat her based on her original gender, and assume she's a girl, in which case I don't have to wear *hijab* around her, and so on, or treat her based on her acquired gender identity and assume she's a boy, in which case I would be accepting something that Islam doesn't condone?"

"Oh God! And how did you respond to this tantalising question?"

"I told her it's neither. She cannot continue to be friends with that person in any capacity, unfortunately."

"How did she take this?"

"Of course she was upset, and asked why my position was so harsh."

"And what did you say?"

"I said listen, if you choose to treat that person as a girl, she would be offended, and if you choose to treat her as a boy, then you cannot Islamically be his friend either!"

"Clever!" He quipped. "Did she accept this answer?"

"She just looked at me with dismay!" I said laughingly.

"Oh man..."

"I made light of the situation by injecting humour and putting a smile on my face, and then I made sure she understood that while she cannot take that person as a friend anymore because of the value set that they have chosen to subscribe to, at the same time she needed to still treat them with compassion, render them advice and be cordial," I said.

"So generally speaking how are we as Muslims supposed to handle the wider social discourse on the transgender movement in light of this perspective?"

"As Western Muslims, we are treading a very fine line. On the one hand, we're required in our faith to adhere to certain boundaries of convictions and forms of behaviour that conform to God's teachings and the overall health and benefit of humanity. On the other hand, we're also expected to treat others with compassion and engage them in ways that would enable us to bring the light of the Quran into their hearts. It has become a challenge to achieve this balance in our modern world. If you oppose homosexuality, gay marriage, and transgender identities, you're deemed a homophobic demagogue, and if you show compassion with whom you disagree with you're considered a sell-out," I said.

"Indeed. I feel this same pain every day."

"And this is why all we need to do is to resort to our Islamic teachings. It is only there that we will find a clear road map. While the scripture is clear about the need to reject obscene and sinful behaviour, God also taught us to hate the sin not the sinner, to treat people with compassion, and to love for others what we love for ourselves. In fact, I believe that if we Muslims made the unprincipled decision of engaging with the LGBTQIA+ community and 'accept' their way of life, we will lose the ability to lend them a helping hand, show them spiritual alternatives, defend their safety, or posit Islam as a relevant force of change in one of the most serious debates of our time. We should work with them, partner with them on matters of concern to the wider society, and maintain good relations with them, while clearly expressing our position on the matter."

"You said 'show them spiritual alternatives', what do you mean by this?" he asked.

"Struggles with sexual orientation, gender identity, and other modern forms of discontent with the self, reflect a wider social phenomenon where people in the West are now being encouraged to subjectively follow their whimsical passions and 'be who they are'. No self-appraisal, no corrective action, no feedback mechanisms, no advice, no mentorship. You can't even counsel someone who has homosexual feelings, or gender confusion and tell them it's okay to feel this way, but it's not okay to make changes in your lifestyle. The modern-day ethos of the LGBTQIA movement relies heavily on silencing any dissent and muffling any opposition," I said.

"The accusation is always ready: you're a homophobic bigot," he said.

"Exactly. And this is not healthy. Not everyone who comes out as gay truly feels that they can't be with the opposite gender. Not everyone who wants to reassign their gender truly and wholeheartedly feels that they're trapped in someone else's body. Sometimes young people want to explore. Sometimes they're bored. Sometimes they're confused. Demanding society to turn itself into a single class of 'yes men' cannot be healthy to anyone," I said.

"But more specifically, what other spiritual choices can we offer people who may experience same-sex desires or gender discontentment?"

"We at least go through the steps I mentioned earlier. Is this a hormonal issue? Is this a genetic issue? Is this a psychological matter? And after that, we can decide. The premature propelling of someone into an acquired sexual orientation or gender identity has caused people to suffer from severe mental health issues and didn't bring relief to their already difficult existence. Saying 'sure!' and being supportive are not always the same thing."

"I heard that many transgender people end up returning to their gender of birth?"

"Indeed. It's called 'detransitioning'. Brown University psychologist Lisa Littman published research suggesting the existence of 'Rapid Onset Gender Dysphoria' in which teenagers make the switch, usually female to male, not as a result of any hormonal issues or a genetically or biologically genuine reason, but through a process of mob mentality, where multiple friends from the same group would undergo the transition, in a way that is statistically impossible. In fact, more than 60% of transgender people now return to their birth gender identity, many after having permanently altered their bodies."

"What a tragedy…" he said while shaking his head in disbelief.

"Without a doubt. Islamic guidance and spiritual alternatives can involve helping struggling youth to think about the matter differently; to realise that while it's okay to feel a certain way, there is no need to make long-term decisions one might regret, or to do something displeasing to God. It needs to be clarified to them that having feelings towards someone of the same sex doesn't necessarily need to translate to sexual relations. They need to be told that it builds character to accept God's decree and endure a trial, rather than caving under pressure etc."

"These are really important thoughts. What practical advice can this dialogue provide to young people who are struggling though?" he asked.

"A few weeks ago, a young Muslim guy in his early 30s, who's relatively observant and really kind, called me with the strangest inquiry."

"What is it?"

"He said on the phone that he's gay, and while he acknowledges who he is and refuses to live a lie by just marrying a woman to satisfy social expectations, he chooses to live as a single man who is not in any relationship with other men."

"This is incredible!"

"That's what I said to him as well. He told me that most Muslims who desire to change their gender or accept their sexual orientation, have been told that there are only two choices: it's either they suppress who they are, get married to someone and try not to think about it, or renounce the faith, fully accept that identity and live that life to its fullest extent. He chose a different path: to accept that he, for now, can't have a viable marriage with a woman, but at the same time to acknowledge that he's not willing to displease God or reject Him. The third path is to forgo sex for the sake of God, as difficult as that is," I said.

"I'm speechless."

"I was too. He even told me that he plans to put together an app, or a social media platform in order to bring together Muslims who may have homosexual feelings but choose to remain Muslim and adhere to orthodoxy, in order to support each other and offer coping mechanisms etc."

"Man! This could be a total game changer! Imagine if the youth are provided with a third option. That would be amazing!" he said.

"I agree. And this is what I meant earlier. That if we give ourselves a chance to accept God's decree and surrender to it, and be honest with ourselves and God, and avoid any equivocation about our beliefs and values, and proclaim compassionately who we are and where we stand, we will be doing justice to society and a great service to so many that are struggling with this black and white dichotomous culture in which we live."

"This was so exhilarating. Can't thank you enough for this perspective Imam!"

"Just pray for me and my family," I said.

He went on his way, almost running to his car. I sat for a few more minutes on the bench, taking in as much as I could from the clear morning breeze. I looked at my watch and realised it was almost noon. I made my way to the mosque's fitting rooms, in order to take a shower and catch *dhuhr* prayer.

*Chapter 10*

# Salvation

So many weeks had passed without seeing him. Despite how mentally taxing our conversations had been, I realised that I missed them! It's not often that Imams, or religious leaders in general, engage in dialogue beyond the regular platitudes of ritual and rite. So I decided to pay him a visit.

"Assalamualaikum!" I greeted him at the door.

"Wa alaykum assalam! What a surprise! Please come in!" he said with great jubilation.

I walked to his guest room and sat on one of the comfortable sofas.

"Great to see you! It's been a while. Just thought I'd check on you and the family," I said with a big smile.

"Means a lot to me, Imam! Can't express how grateful I am," he said.

"I have to admit that I have ulterior motives for coming here," I said with an embarrassed chuckle.

"What is it?" he asked with close attention.

"Well, you know, I wanted to follow up on our conversations about God. You know…the ones about your nephew."

"Aha! I've been meaning to follow up with you as well and give you some updates but got busy with family matters. You know what? Let me get you some refreshments first and then we can talk."

"I think I'm good. No need to worry yourself. We can talk now," I said impatiently.

"You taught us that the shortest path to heaven is to honour

our guests, didn't you?" he asked with a smirk.

"Ah yes…sure, please," I said while clearing my throat in embarrassment.

"How do you like your coffee?" he asked.

"Black, please."

He left the room to get some coffee and left me ruminating on my thoughts. I turned my face around the room, and couldn't help but get fixated on a frame hanging on the wall, portraying the old saying by Imam Ali bin Abi Talib in beautiful Arabic calligraphy: 'Knowledge is superior to wealth, for you have to protect wealth, whereas knowledge protects you.'"[64]

"My dad gave this to me," he said as he suddenly entered the room. I was taken by surprise.

"Oh man! You scared me!" I gasped.

"So sorry! Didn't mean to startle you. Was just saying that frame was a gift from my dad."

"It's beautiful, in form and essence."

"I feel the same way. Been on my wall since I got married. It was one of my dad's last wishes for me to keep it in the family and share it with my kids as an heirloom."

"What a thoughtful dad! May God have mercy on his soul."

"Ameen."

"What's the latest and greatest with your nephew?" I asked.

"Well, it's been quite an upheaval with him. This ordeal changed the dynamics of the entire family. I have to say that despite the challenges, we're all better off for it. We think more and ask more. As for my nephew, we've been talking a lot recently. Almost every other day. His questions have become a lot less intense, and his attitude is less belligerent."

"So where do you think he is now in terms of his intellectual journey?"

"I learned from you that my job is to just be kind, share the right knowledge, and leave the rest in the hands of God, so frankly I don't even ask him anymore," he said with ease.

"This is really good. You're making a lot more progress than you think."

"I have a hunch though, that he now cannot completely dismiss the concept of God. He alluded to that multiple times indirectly in our conversations."

"Can't describe how happy I am to hear this," I said with gratitude.

"Everything takes time as you repeatedly said, right?"

"Indeed."

"Last time we met he actually brought up some really good points that I never thought of before. Perhaps we can chat about those?"

I turned in my seat and faced him with great attention.

"Of course! What is it?" I blurted out.

"Glad to see you're the one who's excited this time," he said with a big smirk.

I chuckled.

"Okay, let me get right to it," he said while adjusting his position. "My nephew is still uneasy, and honestly so am I, about salvation," he continued.

"Salvation?" I asked.

"Yes, as in who gets to be saved on the Day of Judgement, in the event that such a thing will actually occur, using my nephew's skeptical words."

"You mean what good deeds will grant us salvation?"

"No. Salvation in the sense of who has the truth. There are so many religious paths in the world. All of them lay claims to the truth. All of them instruct their followers every day that the path to salvation is exclusively achieved through following the tenets of *their* religion. Everyone says everyone else is going to hell. How can we choose?"

"So the confusion is about the multiplicity of religions?" I asked.

"Pretty much. Jews argue that they are God's own children and chosen people, and if you're any good He would have selected you to be born into Judaism. Christians hold that it is only through believing that God sacrificed his son Jesus Christ on the cross, that salvation is attained. Muslims make it very clear that you have to accept the Prophet Muhammad as the final prophet, and the Quran as the word of God, to be saved. Buddhists, Taoists, Hindus, and others all have their own views and claims of salvation. If God does exist, my nephew asks, first: why did He allow for so many religions to develop? Why not just one religion? Second, how can a sincere seeker choose between all these paths? Third, what happens to those who didn't follow a religion because they didn't have prophets or messengers? Fourth, what happens to righteous people who may have followed the wrong religion because they don't know better?" he asked.

"I see. Interesting questions," I said while nodding and then gazed into the distance through his guest room window.

"Where did you go?" he asked.

"Nowhere. Just trying to organise my thoughts to address these fundamental questions. I think we have to first break down the questions, and then point out flaws in the assumptions they make, before I address them. Fair?"

"Fair."

"Okay. So the core point made here is that there are many religions in the world with claims to salvation, making it difficult for someone to decide which one to follow. Is this accurate?" I asked.

"I think so, yes," he responded.

"First, let me ask you this: if God does exist, which as believers we answer in the affirmative, how would He communicate His instructions and injunctions to humanity?"

"Through prophets, messengers, and scriptures, I suppose."

"Precisely. And since people throughout history lived in different locations, with different languages, cultures, and internal challenges, what was necessary in order for everyone to hear the message of God?"

"Well, to send multiple prophets, I presume."

"Great. And since people lived in different time frames, and considering that humanity evolves, and its problems evolve with it, what is also necessary?"

"That a succession of prophets and messengers are sent across the centuries."

"Wonderful! So we agree that if God exists, and if He has instructions for us, which seems like the most plausible assumption, He would send prophets and messengers with divine guidance, to all kinds of people, in their localities, speaking their languages, across time and geographical regions, right?" I asked.

"I agree with that," he responded.

"Now let me ask you: when a given prophet is sent to a small village somewhere, with local problems that he needed to address, over which he'd bring divine guidance to bear, and when those local problems haven't spread somewhere else, what would the mission of that prophet constitute?"

"Not sure..."

"It would be a local mission, to serve a local group, with local problems, and the mandate would end by the expiration of that prophet, wouldn't you say?"

"Indeed! My dad used to talk to me about the difference between prophets and messengers, and that a prophet is sent to a small group, but a messenger is a prophet who brings a scriptural message from God in the form of an actual book of guidance and would essentially found a new religion," he said.

"I agree with your first point about the difference between prophets and messengers, but it's not necessarily true that every messenger who was sent with a divine book founded a new religion."

"Fascinating! But Moses brought the Torah and founded Judaism, and Jesus brought the *Injil*, or the New Testament of the Bible, and founded Christianity, and Muhammad brought the Quran, and founded Islam, right?"

"Dangerously wrong!"

"You're doing it again."

"What?"

"Dismantling my age-old beliefs."

"It's what I do," I said with a mischievous smile, "Think about it. What was Dawud's book?"

"*Zaboor.*"

"What religion did Dawud organise?"

"Uhm...I don't know. He was a prophet in the succession of other Hebrew prophets I believe."

"What about Ibrahim's book?"

"The *Suhuf* right?"

"Yes, but which religion did he organise?"

"Don't know."

"None of these messengers organised new religions. That's the point. Although God sent them with scriptures, it didn't necessarily signal the founding of new religions."

"I see. So just major religions, such as Judaism, Christianity, Hinduism etc, right?" he asked.

"With qualifications, but we'll talk about that later. For now, we agree that God sent prophets with a more limited mandate to address local issues with smaller human communities, and sent messengers with a bigger mandate to larger groups, right?"

"I think that's what I gathered so far."

"Great. Is there anything unfair about this process?"

"I wouldn't think so."

"So in essence, what we're saying is that there's nothing wrong with the multiplicity of religious paths, correct?"

"Well, only when they're unfolding at different places but still within the same time frame. But when they linger across time, muster followers who come into direct contact with each other, and start fighting with one another, and claim that everyone else is going to hell for not following *their* path, that's when we start having problems," he said.

"That's a great point. I might have a resolution for this, and I'll address it later, but for now, let's examine the claims to salvation that different religions make."

"I'm listening attentively!"

"Great. In your nephew's questions, he was particularly troubled by the fact that every religion presumably proclaims that only its own followers will go to heaven and everyone else that doesn't follow them is not, right?"

"Yes."

"Let me go ahead and say that this assumption is not true. Not all religions make that claim."

"Wow…I didn't know that. So some religions don't claim that only their followers are going to heaven?"

"Yes. Many of them don't. In fact, when it comes to claims to salvation, people assume that religions are roughly divided into three groups. The exclusivist group, the inclusivist group, and the hybrid group."

"What are these?" he asked impatiently.

"Well, let's take them one by one. I see that you're the one who is becoming impatient now!" I said with a mischievous chuckle.

"Forgive me. Okay. I'll control myself," he said with a nervous laugh.

"Alright great. The first group is the exclusivist group. In this perspective, followers of a particular religious doctrine or religion believe that only they will be saved and will go to heaven. This represents what your nephew was asking about it, but obviously, it's not the only group."

"Yes. This is the most popular group. Most people think that this is how religions are."

"Indeed. I'm aware of this. This is why we have to discuss this group first since it's the most common."

"So basically for them, anyone, even the kindest and most charitable members of another faith are still doomed to hell, right?" he asked.

"Right. It's the belief that deeds are not sufficient to attain sal-

THE IMAM AND THE ATHEIST

vation. Following true faith and believing in the right doctrine matter the most. If you are the most amazing human being but worship the wrong god or worship the right one through the wrong set of rituals, you are still doomed," I answered.

"Sounds harsh. My nephew was asking me the other day: 'If you believe in the Christian God, why would Gandhi go to hell? And if you believe in the Muslim God, why would Mother Theresa go to hell'?"

"I'm familiar with these questions and have received them before, and they are valid. Not everyone on earth will get to know God the same way a particular group in a particular place within a particular time frame would. I can certainly see why this would bother many," I said.

"It bothers me a bit too. So which religions believe in this exclusive salvation doctrine?"

"Many. Most Christian denominations argue that one has to accept Jesus Christ as the Son of God and the Saviour who died on the cross for our sins in order to be saved. In fact, many Catholic mothers rush from the hospital to the church in order to baptise their newborn babies for fear that if the baby died for any reason before baptism it might not be saved on Judgement Day."

"Wow."

"Most traditional Christianity holds dear the notion that salvation is only obtained through Jesus Christ. Catholics, Evangelicals, Lutherans, and more conservative denominations are very exclusivist."

"Interesting. What about Muslims and Jews?"

"Most Muslims believe in this exclusive salvation as well. Orthodox and most conservative Jews hold a similar view. It's interesting that in Judaism, the notion of exclusive salvation takes its most extreme form."

"How?" he asked curiously.

"The assumption is not only that Jews will go to heaven, but that if there's any good in you God would have selected you among

His chosen people. Everyone else pretty much stands no chance for salvation," I answered.

"But this is not what all Jews believe, is it?"

"As I said, Orthodox and most conservative Jews abide by this doctrine."

"I can see how this doctrine can make things easy for the followers of a particular faith. But for others, it obviously makes no sense. Those who are not born into that faith and didn't have proper exposure to its teachings will definitely protest its exclusive claim to salvation, and will either push back by claiming exclusive salvation to their own faith or losing trust in religion altogether."

"And we see the latter happening now more often than not. Young people, especially those who grew up in pluralistic and diverse societies, are having a hard time accepting that salvation, if God exists, is exclusive to one particular group and that everyone else is going to hell, just because they were not raised by the right family, didn't grow up in the right culture and didn't practice the right religion."

"Disturbing. So where do other religious groups stand with regards to salvation then?" he asked.

"Well, the second group is predictably the inclusivist group. They arose as a direct reaction to the exclusivist group. Members of many faiths couldn't accept that salvation is monopolised by one faith group, but they couldn't reject the concept of God either. So they ended up developing a doctrine that God revealed Himself to the righteous through many, if not all faiths. In this understanding, virtually all faiths will ultimately lead to salvation."

"All faiths?"

"Most, I should say. In this understanding, the core message of all religions is the same, but the details are taught differently from one faith to the other. The core message of all religions is to be in harmony with God, the universe, and your fellow man, to live a moral life, to honour God and family etc. Those teachings are echoed in every religion, even if the details of ritual and rite are different," I elaborated.

"So according to this understanding, all religions are right?"

"Pretty much, with reservations obviously."

"Like what?"

"For instance, devil-worshipping would not be included here. Neither are sects or cults that spring out here and there to serve the agendas of particularly deranged individuals."

"But who's to say which path is a cult and which is the true religion? Christianity and Islam sure looked like cults in their early days," he said.

"Great point, and it's one of the reasons this doctrine is also heavily critiqued. If all paths presumably lead to God, which is included and which is not? And on what basis can we decide?"

"Exactly."

"More importantly, if all paths lead to salvation, then what's the point of joining any? I can just keep switching every day. I can attend *Jumuah* on a given Friday, and the following week attend the Sabbath service on Saturday, and the third week attend Mass on Sunday."

"Yep. That would not make sense. But in addition to that, religions, although they might agree on certain core principles and core ethics, still conflict in terms of prohibitions and permissibilities. While eating pork, for example, is wrong in one faith, it's acceptable in another. Which should I follow?"

"Great point. And if all paths are right, then what's the point of studying the creed or theology of a particular religion? What's the point of ordainment? And what's the point of ritual worship?"

"There would be no point for sure. Which religious groups are considered inclusivist?" he asked.

"The Unitarian Church, many Hindu groups, and some Perennialist sects are considered inclusivists."

"Oh, man. But this complicates things. If neither exclusivity nor inclusivity is working, then where do we go from here?"

"Well, that's why a third group evolved!"

"A third group? Don't tell me! A hybrid between the two?"

"Good guess!" I said with a laugh.

"Man. How does that work?"

"Well, it's sort of an intermediary path, where it is assumed that God may have revealed Himself in different paths and that bits of relative spiritual truth reside in multiple religions, but ultimately there's one absolute truth that is embodied in the teachings of one religion."

"Aha! That is clever!" he said with bright eyes.

"Indeed, at least in the minds of the followers of this doctrine. Many liberal Christian groups such as Episcopalians and Methodists accept this notion. While the path to salvation essentially goes through accepting Jesus Christ as your saviour, they acknowledge that some will still be saved even if they don't accept Christ, considering that they didn't have proper exposure or comprehension of who he is, or what his example was about."

"This sounds very interesting. Can this potentially address the claims of atheists about salvation?"

"No, it can't. Very legitimate questions are raised that can potentially be fatal to this doctrine."

"Like what?!"

"For example, which path would be considered the absolute truth? And on what basis will that be decided? And if there's truth in other faiths, then what's the point of actually searching for the absolute truth? And if searching for the absolute truth is valuable in and of itself, then on what basis can the veracity of such claims be established? And if I somehow found a way to verify the claims of one faith to be true, what about sects and subgroups within that faith? If Christianity is the right path that bears the absolute truth, then should one be Catholic or Protestant? And if you choose to be Protestant, which of the further fragmentations of Protestant Christianity should one follow? Lutheran? Methodist? And so on," I stated.

"Good grief! Where do we go from here then? You said there

are only three choices, and if all three of them don't work, then what can we say to someone like my nephew?"

"I didn't say there are only three choices. I just said it is what people assume."

"Wait...Are you saying there's a fourth path?"

"Yes. And it's the one that makes the most sense."

"Please tell me! Which one is that?" he asked impatiently.

"Well, before I do this, let's first discuss the meaning of religion."

"What do you mean?"

"I'm referring to the word 'religion' and its connotations."

"Okay. How's this relevant to our debate?"

"Very relevant. You see, the word religion in and of itself implies exclusivity, no matter how you spin it. Once I utter 'religion' it automatically implies a clearly distinct set of beliefs, rituals, practices, dos and don'ts, that are clearly demarcated from other 'religions'. In other words, no matter what we do, the concerns your nephew has about the claims made by different 'religions' about salvation cannot be adequately addressed, because the very existence of multiple paths is confusing, whether they are exclusivist, inclusivist, or a hybrid of both," I said.

"Exactly. That's what's so frustrating. If only there was just one religion!"

"Well, there are many religions for sure, but there has to be only one true way of life that leads to God."

"What do you mean by this?"

"What I mean is that religion is part-divine part-man, while the true way of life is entirely divine."

"You keep using the word 'way of life'. How is that different from religion? And why do you say that religion is part-man?"

"Because it is. Think about it. God revealed scriptures, teachings, and instructions to His prophets and messengers, and over time, the scriptures are lost, and the teachings are altered. A certain path to God may have originated a certain way, but it then changes so significantly over time that what ends up in our hands, while tracing its roots back to divine inspiration, is riddled with human intervention, additions, and alterations. Religion, as is understood today, is a combination of those two components."

"So…what's the way out of this?"

"To search for a path that didn't undergo this process. A path that has always been there from the beginning. A path that regardless of what has occurred throughout the centuries remains unchanged and unaltered. A path that was the foundation of every divine message, every scripture, and every prophetic mission."

"And what is that path exactly?" he asked.

"Allow me to ask you this: you claim to be Muslim. On what basis do you think that Islam is the true path?"

"Well, because it's the only religion that has fewer contradictions."

"Religion? See that's the problem right there."

"What?"

"Islam is not a religion as understood in Western perceptions. It's a way of life that predates the advent of what Westerners would consider to be its founder."

"The Prophet Muhammad?"

"Yes. But not just the Prophet. Islam 'the way of life', or using Quranic terminology, the '*deen*', predates Islam the 'religion'," I said.

"I'm super confused right now. Didn't you say that Islam was not a religion?"

"Yes, but in the mind of most of its followers, and most non-Muslims, Islam is just 'another' religion."

"Is it not?"

"No. It is not. Here's a useful way to think of this. Consider horses, for instance."

"Horses?" he asked.

"Yes. Horses. There are so many of them. Big and small, fast and slow, wild and domesticated. There are modern horses and prehistoric horses. They live in different places and perform different functions. They may look very different from each other, but at the end of the day, no matter how different they are, they're still horses, right?"

"Yes..."

"With the same token, I want you to think about God's path and His teachings as He packaged them to humanity from the dawn of time. That God's path, that way of life, that '*deen*' has always been Islam, in its strictest sense, which is 'to surrender yourself to the will of God', and not necessarily in its theological sense to denote the followers of the Prophet Muhammad who believe in the validity of the Quran."

"I think I understand this. So God's way has always been Islam from day one?" he asked.

"Indeed. Islam, with a capital 'I', has, and will always be the way of life, the true path, and the *deen* of God. Throughout the centuries, God would reveal components of His teachings through scriptures, prophets, and messengers, saying the same thing and instructing their followers to follow pretty much the same rules."

"Is this why the Quran considers Adam to be a prophet?"

"Exactly. And not just a prophet. The Quran also considers him a Muslim, in the historic sense of the word."

"I think I'm beginning to follow what you're saying here. So this is why the Quran also considers the followers of Noah, Moses, and Jesus to be Muslims?"

"Precisely! Those who followed their prophets until the message of God was 'updated' through the subsequent revelation are strictly Muslim," I said.

"So if the followers of Moses were Muslim, what about those who followed Jesus?" he asked.

"Well, those who followed Moses were Muslim. When Jesus arrived, those who followed him continued to be Muslim. In other words, the followers of Moses who didn't follow Jesus became Jews, and that's how the 'religion' of Judaism was created, through this process of rejection."

"So what you're saying is that it was Jesus that founded Judaism?"

"Well, not exactly!" I said with a laugh, but continued: "Judaism was rather founded by those who used to be Muslim by following Moses, but refused to follow Jesus."

"This is an astounding way of looking at things. What about Christians?"

"Well, prior to the Prophet Muhammad, those who truly followed Christ as a Prophet and a human were also considered Muslims, but when the Prophet Muhammad was sent with the Quran as the final revelation, those who refused to follow him after hearing about his message, ended up precipitating the events that created what we today call Christianity."

"This is mind-boggling!" he cried.

"Not if you grasp it fully."

"So...what about those we call Muslim today?"

"Well, as I said, Islam didn't start with the Prophet Muhammad, in fact, it was 'sealed' through his prophethood. But today's followers of the Prophet Muhammad are Muslims, in both the historic and the theological sense, meaning they surrender themselves to the Will of God, but also follow the teachings of the final chapter in God's message to humanity, also known as the Quran."

"This is incredible. But why does this address the variety of religious paths and the claims to salvation?" he asked.

"Well, it's the only perspective that does. Earlier I said people assume there are only three different types of ways to look at salvation: the exclusivist, the inclusivist, and the hybrid, right?"

"Yes."

"What I'm saying is that Islam offers a fourth way of looking at things. If the only way of life, the only '*deen*' has always been Islam, in the historic sense, then all 'religions' were just manifestations of that Islam, that served important purposes. Islams with a small 'i' if you will. The last installment, the final chapter so to speak in God's story, was the Quran as revealed through the Prophet

Muhammad. This eliminates the confusion of multiple 'religions', or at least it confines the word religion to a temporary system of thought and ritual that perhaps has divine roots, but still riddled with human ideas and alterations. There is one way of life; one *deen*, and this establishes that the path to God is only one."

"I'm speechless…"

"You see, the Quran states this time and time again. Muslims are required to accept biblical prophets as true apostles, and to respect the Torah and the Bible as scriptures, even if they believe that they have been altered over time. Muslims don't ask Jews and Christians to forgo the teachings of their 'religions' but to complete them by accepting the Quran, so that 'religion' becomes 'a way of life' or a '*deen*' as I clarified earlier."

"So you're saying that non-Muslims who follow other religions are not necessarily infidels?"

"They indeed aren't. More like 'incomplete Muslims' if you will."

"But without the nuance of your clarifications and distinctions, doesn't this understanding make it sound like Islam lays an exclusive claim to salvation?"

"In order to make an exclusivist claim to anything, you have to have multiple choices. What I'm saying is there isn't. It's only one *deen*. But I'm not arguing for the validity of Islam right now. Perhaps this should be the subject of another dialogue between us. I'm just sharing with you that there is a fourth way to look at salvation."

"Be that as it may, the problem still remains, I think. You're saying that Islam, with a capital 'I', has always been God's '*deen*', or way of life. Every authentic 'religion' has divine roots but was altered over time and the only one that wasn't is Islam. Ultimately though, what you're saying to those who don't follow today's Islam is that they won't be saved. What you're telling them is that it is only through accepting the Prophet Muhammad and the Quran that you can attain salvation, right?"

"Correct," I affirmed.

"Then how is this not an exclusivist position?"

"Because an exclusivist position contends that all others who don't follow it are necessarily going to hell."

"Is this not what we're saying?"

"Not entirely. Look here: scholars have addressed this dilemma across the centuries. One of the most profound takes on it was propounded by Imam Ghazali. Ibn-Taymiyah also addressed it but with less force. According to Ghazali, people, when it comes to faith, are divided into five categories, according to Islamic theology. The first group is the followers of Muhammad, or Muslims with a small 'm', who accepted the Quran and practice the rites of Islam after the advent of the Prophet Muhammad. They will be saved from eternal damnation, but some of them might have to do time in hellfire to atone for their sins unless God envelops them with his mercy."

"This makes sense. What about the second group?"

"Well, the second group is any non-Muslim who follows the scriptures of the people of the book, and never heard of Islam because they lived in remote lands and were never exposed to the teachings of the Prophet Muhammad."

"And what becomes of those?"

"Imam Ghazali says that they will be covered by God's mercy and will be excused for their ignorance."

"Okay, this is very interesting. What's the third category?"

"It's that of people who actually heard of Islam, the Prophet Muhammad or the Quran, but were told their entire lives that Muhammad was a bad man and that the Quran is evil. It was very difficult for them to get a clear measure of the Prophet's life or an honest demonstration of Islamic teachings."

"And how will God treat those?"

"Imam Ghazali says that they will likely be forgiven and saved as well, as long as they were true to the authentic teachings of their scriptures and did what they could to abide by them."

"Well, this is a game-changer! This probably applies to so many non-Muslims today who live a life of kindness and piety. It would feel unfair if they ended up in hell!"

"Fair and unfair are determined by the Creator. My job here is to answer your questions," I said with a smirk.

"Fair enough," he said with a smile. "What's the fourth group then?"

"The fourth group is those who have had proper exposure to Islam and the teachings of the Prophet Muhammad, in a way that piqued their curiosity, and compelled them to embark upon a journey of investigation to study Islam, but passed away before actually becoming Muslims."

"This is fascinating! And what did Ghazali say about their destiny?"

"He also argued that they will be enveloped by God's mercy since they were already on their path."

"This is amazing and heartwarming! What an exhilaration to realise how nuanced and sophisticated our classical scholars were!"

"Indeed," I followed.

"What about the fifth category?"

"The fifth group according to Ghazali is non-Muslims who have had the proper exposure to Islam and knew about the Prophet Muhammad's life, and Islamic teachings actually made sense to them, but they refused to follow those teachings for one reason or another."

"I think I can guess what becomes of those."

"What?" I asked.

"I think they won't be saved," he said with hesitation.

"Good guess. Those are considered *kuffar*, or infidels, disbelievers, rejecters of the truth, as the word implies, and those are the ones that will be doomed in the afterlife."

"Man…I'm super delirious right now, with all this eye-opening information."

"You're welcome," I said.

"Wait! With all this in mind, can I assume that my neighbour, who has known me for 30 years, and came to our mosque many times, and read the Quran, and attended interfaith events, and had the most amazing connection with our Muslim community for decades, but still is a practicing Christian, is going to hell?" he said with a horrified voice.

"Be careful there. It's one thing to designate abstract categories, but Imam Ghazali warns against speaking on God's behalf and deciding who goes to heaven and who goes to hell. If we cannot make that determination with regards to ourselves, then we shouldn't make it about others."

"Makes perfect sense. These matters will be decided on the Day of Judgement."

"Exactly."

"This was amazing and exciting as usual!"

"Thank you! I'm grateful for your amazing hospitality. Thank you for having me," I said as I got ready to leave his house.

"You're welcome! Anytime. Let's meet up soon. I will surely relay today's dialogue to my nephew."

"Do that, and pray for me."

"Will do."

He walked me up to the door, opened it, and suddenly gave me a tight hug, and said: "I can't thank you enough," he said emotionally.

"I should thank *you* for giving me a chance to affirm my faith in the Creator," I responded nervously. I then walked through the door, glanced at his face, and said: "Assalamualaikum"

"Wa alaykum assalam."

## Chapter 11

# Conclusions

It was an exceptionally pleasant Saturday morning. The sun reflected gorgeously on the pond behind my house, and the birds kept chirping and hopping between the fruit trees in the orchard. The sky was clear like a big blue ocean, and in the distance, I could see the mountain line, still covered with a snow cap. I stood on my patio filling my eyes with this scene, with a smile of gratitude on my face and a freshly brewed coffee mug in my hand, taking deep breaths and trying to keep the fresh air in my chest for as long as I could. It was a little decadent desire of mine, to enjoy the morning sunshine before the kids were awake. I slowly walked on my lawn towards the end of the yard, where a concrete set of benches is situated to get the best view of the mountains. I sat there mesmerised, observing God's creation. I usually delay turning on my phone in the morning for as long as I can, to enjoy my morning before the barrage of messages and notifications come down like a merciless flood. I stared at my phone for a second, debating whether I should turn it on or not. Finally, I decided to see what the world was up to. Notification after notification poured in. I sat my phone on the table and continued to sip my coffee. After a minute or so, the notification sounds died down. I picked up my phone, unlocked it, and took a quick glance at the notification bar. Mostly mundane stuff, but one text message particularly grasped my attention immediately.

"Imam, didn't want to wake you, but I'm outside in my car, with my nephew. He finally expressed his desire to meet you. I didn't want to waste any time. Let me know when you're up!"

I sat there in astonishment.

He's here, in my court, I thought to myself, baffled. But then I realised that it's against all the simple rules of courtesy that my dad and my Imam taught me, to leave my guests sitting in a car outside my house. I grabbed my coffee, walked towards the side door of my backyard, all the way to my court, and saw them, sitting in a silver car in front of the main entrance of the house.

"Assalamualaikum and welcome!" I said with an amused voice and a big smile on my face.

"Wa alaykum assalam!" they both said with almost the same voice as they enthusiastically exited their vehicle.

"So sorry if we interrupted your morning without a prior appointment!" said the uncle apologetically.

"No worries at all! You're always welcome here, with or without an appointment," I said warmly. I then turned my eyes onto the younger of the two. He was not anything like I imagined. I always thought of him as a short guy, wearing glasses, displaying an erratic attitude. Despite my prejudice, he was at least 6 ft. tall, well-built, and without any glasses. There was a humble confidence about his demeanour that intrigued me. I addressed him and said: "You must be the nephew!"

"That'll be me!" he said with a smile.

"Please, do come in," I said as I walked towards the front door. I arrived at the door and tried to open it, but it was locked from the inside. "Oh shoot! Sorry guys! The door is closed. I came from the backyard!" I said nervously.

"Oh no worries!" the uncle said.

"Please, walk with me. Let's sit in the backyard. It's beautiful back there!" I said while walking towards the backyard's side door. They walked with me, and we made our way to my spot at the very back, and I gestured to them to sit down and said: "Please, have a seat!" They both sat down and looked with amusement at the mountain line on the horizon. The nephew said: "The view here is breathtaking!"

"Well, it's one of the greatest blessings of life for me to sit here, have some coffee and enjoy this view. Speaking of coffee, let me get you some fresh brew!" I said.

"I'll have some!" the uncle said.

"No coffee for me. Water would be enough. Thank you!" said the nephew.

"One coffee and one water coming right up!" I said with a big smile, as I walked to the house. I was intrigued but also a tad apprehensive that the nephew came all the way to my house. Only months ago he was barely talking to his family, and now he has no problem talking to the Imam, at his house? I wasn't sure what all that meant, but I figured he's at my house and he deserves my hospitality. I grabbed a mug of fresh coffee, and a glass of ice water, put them on a tray, and walked towards my early morning guests.

"There you go, guys!" I said, as I put the tray on the table.

"Thank you, Imam," they said.

I realised that I was still holding my mug, so I took a sip after I sat down, and looked at them both with a smile.

"Imam, my nephew is here because he has a few questions," the uncle said.

"Actually, I'm here mostly because I wanted to meet you first and foremost. But yes, I do have a couple of questions as well," the nephew said.

"Well, I hope our first encounter was not underwhelming!" I said with a loud laugh.

"If you only knew how much I thought of you the last few weeks," the nephew said with enthusiasm. "I just wanted to meet the Imam-philosopher! We don't have many of them these days!" he continued with a smile of gratitude.

"Imam-philosopher! That's a good one," I burst out laughing. "Don't hear that very often," I said through my laughter.

"I'm serious. You effectively changed all my perceptions about and exposed all my biases against religious leaders."

"I'm humbled. Tell me a little about yourself."

"I'm sure there's nothing about me that my uncle hasn't already shared," he said with a laugh.

"Touché!" I said with a grin.

"Imam, my nephew asked me many times before about your education. He was surprised by how diverse your knowledge is. Did you study philosophy formally?" asked the uncle.

"I'm humbled. I took philosophy classes at both the undergraduate and graduate levels, although most of my knowledge about philosophy is self-taught, and is driven by the desire to find answers to man's pertinent questions," I answered.

"And what are those?" the uncle asked.

"Well, questions such as: who are we? Where do we come from? How did life start on earth? How did the universe begin? Does God exist? Which religion is the true path? etc."

"But you're a man of faith, and an Imam. Why did you feel the need to use philosophy to get those questions answered, when you could have just relied on the standard answers within religion?" asked the nephew.

"Well, this meeting right here is an answer to your question."

"How so?"

"Had I settled for the conventional religious answers to those questions, I wouldn't have been of any value to you, would I?"

"You got me there!" the nephew said with amusement.

"You see, most religious leaders of today have little knowledge of philosophy for many reasons. First, they think it's just esoteric arguments and impractical contentions that bring no value to man's real problems and challenges. Second, they're mostly content, like you alluded to earlier, with cliché answers that reside in religious dogma. Third, they're busy with the day to day struggles of their congregations, and have no time to engage in the necessary mental grind that characterises existential dilemmas. These factors left faith leaders and their followers not only vulnerable, but completely defenceless against the rapid evolution of material and naturalistic thought that has come to define the modern age," I said.

"I appreciate your analysis. But is it possible that the reason religious leaders are not engaged in philosophical discussions is because religion is self-absorbed by its own dogma and lacks, by definition, the necessary conceptual pliability that is a necessary condition for philosophy?" the nephew asked respectfully.

"Perhaps this applies to some religious traditions. In my judgement though, the question is not whether religious belief has room for philosophical debates. It's mainly whether philosophy can give us an insight into whether religious belief is plausible or not."

"So, whether philosophy can prove or disprove religion?"

"More like: whether philosophy can exclude all the impossible options."

"Got it. I'm familiar with your view on this matter, through my conversations with my uncle. But I want to go back to your point about religious leaders lacking in any philosophical inclinations. What do you think this has done to modern religion?" he asked.

"Religion by definition is an institution of ideas that is bestowed from the Divine unto human beings. This institution should be immutable in its dogma, perceptions of God, and views on the hereafter etc. but it certainly must be adaptable to the times in terms of its social and behavioural mandate."

"Can you elaborate here?"

"What I'm saying is that religion regulates two different domains: the transcendental and the mundane. It's only the otherworldly that should be stable and resistant to change, because that involves dogma that is very foundational to religion. But the impact that religion has on society, and how it tackles evolving social challenges, and how it informs political and economic decisions, needs to adapt to changing times, in order for religion to have any relevance. And I'm not suggesting that religion needs to change its views on right or wrong, rather, it needs to have a view about novel challenges so that they can be categorised as right or wrong."

"Can you give an example?" he asked.

"Well, religion would argue that fornication and adultery are wrong, but in modern times, society needs more guidance on matters of sexual misconduct that are more layered and complicated, such as the consumption of porn, what constitutes sexual harassment, spousal rape, underage sex, trafficking, sex change etc. And I don't mean just issuing a religious opinion on these matters, but also making a case to the public that renders the religious position reasonable and plausible even for non-religious people."

"I see your point, and that is where philosophical debates can come in handy, I suppose?"

"Absolutely. The biggest fault of religious leaders in the modern age is that, while they managed to offer plenty of religious guidance to their followers, they failed to synthesise a framework in which faithful people can operate consistently within modernity."

"This is a great point. I think someone like me is likely a casualty of this failure," he said with a nervous chuckle.

"Nothing we can't fix!" I said with a smirk.

"I still have a few more questions if you don't mind."

"By all means!"

"Well, what do you say to someone who argues that we don't need religion anymore, since it has always been associated with violence and carnage. All we need is secular humanism that seems to be the best solution for modernity."

"Great question. I say you probably need to read some literature on the critique of modernity. It's not true that religion brought nothing but violence and blood, while modernity brought peace and prosperity. Imperialism was a product of modernity. Hedonism was a product of modernity. World wars happened within the modern cultural era, and were a direct product of the nation state, another fruit of modernity. Fascism was a product of modernity. The atom bomb was a product of modernity. The overall estrangement of the modern man and the pervasive mental health crisis are also, directly or indirectly, products of modernity. Even phenomena such as mass shootings in America and the confinement of millions of Muslims in Chinese concentration camps are, one way or another, traced to secular modernity. It might be true that religious fanatics were responsible for unspeakable crimes in modern times, from the KKK to Al-Qaeda, but the overall impact of secular violence far surpasses the casualties of religious violence."

"So what do you mean to say?" he asked.

"That the constant removal of religion from public life, the pervasive assault on religion, and the sidelining of religious morality everywhere, may have suspended the natural regulatory effect that religion ought to play in society. Much of our modern crises were precipitated, not as a result of, but for the lack of religious values," I stated.

"Very interesting perspective. But all wars and violence aside, the sidelining of religion contributed directly to the scientific revolution, the enlightenment and the spread of democratic ideals, wouldn't you say?"

"Well, this Hegelian perspective has proven to be faulty. The assumption that the unfolding of history, or the advancement of science somehow leads to a direction of progress cannot be farther from the truth. The scientific revolution led to tremendous injustices. Capitalism led to massive exploitations. The accumulation of wealth led to slavery. Democratic transitions in Europe led to imperialism. Technological advancements led to the internal combustion engine and machinated factories that are destroying the environment and the atom bomb that took hundreds of thousands of lives. Our modern inventions, from smartphones and social media, may have made human life more convenient, but are we necessarily happier?"

"I see that you are a skeptic too," he said with a smile.

"Perhaps. I just wanted to show you that things are not as black and white as some might think. Even if we assume that scientific progress is always good, the sidelining of religion may have been necessary only within the European context perhaps, and not everywhere."

"What do you mean?"

"Well, the enmity between established Christianity in Europe in the Middle Ages and any form of free thought, made the two mutually exclusive, hence it became necessary to neutralise religion if any progress in science, economics or politics were to be achieved. The same was not true in the Muslim world, for instance. Muslim leaders and theologians encouraged scientic research, philosophical debates and the translation of Greek classical works. They were just not given a chance."

"Who didn't give them a chance?"

"European modernists. As democracy and freedom were spreading in Europe, European armies were occupying territories all over the Muslim world. And after the colonists decided to finally exit Muslim countries, they left behind authoritarian regimes in order to rule the colonies by proxy. This continues to be the case to this day. The opportunity for religious thought and social and scientific advancements to coexist and inform each other, was never given a chance."

"So you're saying had the Muslim world not been colonised by Europeans, Islam and modernity would have managed to coexist?"

"I'm saying that it would have led to an experiment in which progress is tempered by faith, not inhibited by it."

"Are you trying to convince me that if I do believe in God, Islam should be my choice?" he asked with a mischievous smile.

"I'm capable of making that argument, but that would require us to have a multitude of meetings."

"Would love to hear more."

"That would be my pleasure!"

"May I ask what piqued your interest in this subject as an Imam?" the nephew asked with great curiosity.

I sighed.

"I hope I didn't cross any line," he said apologetically.

"Not at all, it's just a nostalgic topic," I said.

He remained silent out of respect.

"Well, I was launched to the path of religious scholarship and philosophical inquiry because I had my share of doubts when I was in college," I said.

"Wait…you had doubts about faith?"

"Yes, sir. Not any different from yours."

"And then what happened?"

"My uncle who was very close to me kept having meetings with an insightful Imam, discussing my struggles with him, and relaying their conversations to me. It was my uncle and that great Imam that saved my life. He's been my greatest teacher ever since."

"This is heartwarming. The similarities here are scaring me!" he said nervously.

"Why do you think I was driven to work with you and answer your questions?" I asked rhetorically.

"Well, I can tell you right now that it made a huge difference. I'm looking forward to having more meetings with you!"

"Me too. God bless you."

"You too!"

"Well! We'll let you enjoy the rest of your day then, Imam!" the uncle interjected.

"It was a pleasure having you guys!"

"We'll see ourselves out. Thank you for your hospitality!" the nephew said.

"It was a pleasure. See you guys soon!"

"InshaAllah."

I sat on my bench, gazing at them as they left the backyard, while sipping on what has now become cold coffee, and grabbed a keychain from my pocket, with the word 'hikmah,' engraved on it, and looked at it with gratitude, then put it back in my pocket, walked back to the house, and closed the backyard's french door behind me.

# Postscript

Aristotle argued that God exists because reason entails the presence of an unmoved mover, and he was criticised. Ghazali argued that God exists because there had to be a first cause, and was criticised. Descartes argued that God exists because it's a mathematical imperative, and was criticised. George Berkeley argued that God exists because He's the mind that can conceive of objects before they are processed into ideas by our sense perception, and was criticised. Kant argued that God exists, not as a result of any hypothesis of analytical reasoning, but because of the moral necessity of His existence, and was criticised. They were followed by Pierce, Whitehead, Gödel, Gardner and others who weaved other philosophical arguments for God but also sustained heavy intellectual casualties in its wake. There isn't a single thinker, philosopher, theologian, or metaphysicist who laid down a detailed argument for the existence of a supreme being that has not been mauled by the sharp claws of a self-serving brand of popular philosophy. Yet, no metaphysical idea managed to survive the incessant molestation of philosophy than that of a Creator. The assumption that the universe has a Maker has not been committed to the museum of antiquated human thought, despite the constant battery. It's not a relic of the past, but an instrument of the present. What are we to do with this interminable lust for God?

God may not necessarily be palpable for all in the sounding of the *Shofar* on Rosh Hashanah, or the singing of hymns at a Southern Gospel Church. God may not even be discernible to everyone that hears the *adhan* or listens to the melodic recitations of the Quran. But God is an idea that manifests itself, one way or another, at some point or the other, to everyone. The faithful cling to it for dear life, and the atheist fights it off like the plague. The Abrahamic sings its praises night and day, and the Buddhist unsuccessfully tries to water it down. The Hindu may try to even its impact over multiple deities and the Pantheist senses it in everything. But ultimately, the idea of God occurs to every human being that was, is or will ever be. This intuitive sense of God, we are instructed, is something that must be dismissed as a farce. Yet we can't, even the most sincere among us in their attempt. We may pretend that we have recovered from the indelible mark of a make-believe Creator, or masquerade as pure materialists who have "cleansed" their minds from the "superstitions" of an ancient deity, but in reality, the human mind is capable of ridding itself of God as much as the enamoured is capable of ridding their heart of the delirium of love.

Modern philosophy did what it could, in no modest terms, to take its jabs at God. But God endures. Human behaviour, conduct, laws, norms, ideas, science, and by extension faith, within a certain epoch, are all deeply influenced by the prevailing philosophical institutions of that epoch. Contemporary philosophy, with its postmodern, analytical and continental branches, is essentially a Godless project. This is not meant in any abrasive sense, rather, to denote that modern human thought operates, almost entirely, on premises and foundations that assume the absence of a Creator. This was not the case in the 19th century, when the Kantian revival dominated the philosophical scene, and will certainly not be the case years from today. Resilient ideas operate in a fashion that resembles ebbs and flows. They rise and fall. They even hit and run. And often, they lead us to fight and flight. But one thing is for sure, however: they never die. The idea of God is the most tenacious of all, and it currently awaits a philosophical revolution to put it back on the map of ideational relevance.

With Allah's will, perhaps this book will ignite that spark.

# Endnotes

1   Quran 35:28
2   Quran 2:30
3   Quran 7:54
4   Quran 70:4
5   Quran 32:5
6   Quran 2:30
7   Quran 20:55
8   Quran 7:18
9   Quran 2:30
10  Quran 15:26-28
11  Quran 3:33
12  Quran 20:122
13  Quran 7:11
14  Quran 2:38
15  Quran 17:85
16  Quran 2:3
17  Quran 53:39
18  Quran 13:27
19  Quran 4:115
20  Quran 18:29
21  Quran 77:30
22  Quran 40:8
23  Quran 6:125
24  Quran 13:39
25  اللهم إن كنت كتبتني في السعداء فأثبتني في السعداء؛ فإنك تمحو ما تشاء وتثبت وعندك أم الكتاب
26  اللهم إن كنت كتبتني شقيا فامحني واكتبني سعيدا، فإنك تمحو ما تشاء وتثبت
27  واصرف عنا شر ما قضيت
28  أنا عند حسن ظن عبدي بي
29  Quran 26:30

30 عن عبد الله بن مسعود قال: حدثنا رسول الله صلى الله عليه وسلم وهو الصادق المصدوق:"إن أحدكم يجمع خلقه في بطن أمه أربعين يومًا نطفة، ثم يكون علقة مثل ذلك، ثم يكون مضغة مثل ذلك، ثم يرسل إليه الملك فينفخ فيه الروح، ويؤمر بأربع كلمات: بكتب رزقه، وأجله، وعمله، وشقي أو سعيد. فوالذي لا إله غيره إن أحدكم ليعمل بعمل أهل الجنة، حتى ما يكون بينه وبينها إلا ذراع، فيسبق عليه الكتاب، فيعمل بعمل أهل النار فيدخلها، وإن أحدكم ليعمل بعمل أهل النار، حتى ما يكون بينه وبينها إلا ذراع، فيسبق عليه الكتاب، فيعمل بعمل أهل الجنة فيدخلها"

31 يكتب

32 Quran 43:32

33 Quran 11:6

34 إنَّ رُوحَ القُدسِ نَفَثَ في رُوعِي أنه لن تَمُوتَ نفس حتى تستكمل رِزْقها (Ahmad)

35 لَوْ تَوَكَّلُونَ عَلَى اللَّهِ حَقَّ تَوَكُّلِهِ ، لَرَزَقَكُمُ اللَّهُ كَمَا يَرْزُقُ الطَّيْرَ ، تَغْدُو خِمَاصًا ، وَتَعُودُ بِطَانًا (Ibn-Hibban)

36 وإن العبد ليحرم الرزق بالذنب يصيبه (Ibn-Majah)

37 Quran 71:4

38 Quran 7:34

39 ولكل أمة أجل

40 Quran 63:11

41 Quran 35:11

42 Quran 6:2

43 ولا يرد القدر إلا الدعاء، ولا يزيد في العمر إلا البر
(in Tirmidhi, Ibn-Majah and Ahmad)

44 من سره أن يبسط له رزقه، وينسأ له في أثره فليصل رحمه

45 صِلَةُ الرَّحِمِ ، وَحُسْنُ الخُلُقِ ، وَحُسْنُ الجِوَارِ ، يُعَمِّرَانِ الدِّيَارَ ، وَيَزِيدَانِ فِي الأَعْمَارِ (Ibn Al-Jawzi)

46 تنبيه الافاضل على ماورد في زيادة العمر ونقصانه من الدلائل (Shawkani)

47 عُمْر

48 إن الله تجاوز لأمتي عما وسوست أو حدثت به أنفسها ما لم تعمل به أو تكلم (Bukhari)

49 أمرد

50 Quran 7:80-81

51 لَعَنَ اللَّهُ مَنْ عَمِلَ عَمَلَ قَوْمِ لُوطٍ (Ahmad)

52 Quran 7:81

53 Quran 29:29

54 Quran 11:78

55 Quran 23:6

56 Quran 5:45

57 Quran 24:31

58 الخنثى المشكل

59  تشبه

60  Quran 53:50

61  لعن المتشبهين من الرجال بالنساء ، والمتشبهات من النساء بالرجال (Bukhari)

62  A person one cannot marry

63  The parts of the body that cannot be exposed except to a person who is a *Mahram*

64  العلم خير من المال العلم يحرسك وأنت تحرس المال